COMPREHENSIVE RESEARCH
AND STUDY GUIDE

# BLOOM'S
## *MAJOR*
# SHORT STORY
### *WRITERS*

# *James* *Joyce*

EDITED AND WITH AN
INTRODUCTION BY HAROLD BLOOM

# CURRENTLY AVAILABLE

COMPREHENSIVE RESEARCH
AND STUDY GUIDE

# BLOOM'S
## *MAJOR*
# SHORT STORY
## *WRITERS*

James
Joyce

EDITED AN                                    BLOOM

Printed and bound in the United States of America.

3 5 7 9 8 6 4 2


Library of Congress Cataloging-in-Publication Data

James Joyce / edited and with an introduction by Harold Bloom.
cm. – (Bloom's major short story writers)
Includes bibliographical references and index.
ISBN 0-7910-5127-7 (hc)
Joyce, James, 1882-1941—Criticism an interpretation—
Handbooks, manuals, etc.    2. Joyce, James, 1882-1941—
Examinations—Study guides.    3. Short Story—Examinations—Study
guides.    4. Short story—Handbooks, manuals, etc.
I. Bloom, Harold.    II. Series.
PR6019.O9Z6335    1998
823.'912—dc21
98-48533
CIP


Chelsea House Publishers
1974 Sproul Road, Suite 400
Broomall, PA 19008-0914


Contributing Editor: Pearl James

# Contents

# User's Guide

This volume is designed to present biographical, critical, and bibliographical information on the author's best-known or most important short stories. Following Harold Bloom's editor's note and introduction is a detailed biography of the author, discussing major life events and important literary accomplishments. A plot summary of each short story follows, tracing significant themes, patterns, and motifs in the work, and an annotated list of characters supplies brief information on the main characters in each story.

A selection of critical extracts, derived from previously published material from leading critics, analyzes aspects of each short story. The extracts consist of statements from the author, if available, early reviews of the work, and later evaluations up to the present. A bibliography of the author's writings (including a complete list of all books written, cowritten, edited, and translated), a list of additional books and articles on the author and the work, and an index of themes and ideas in the author's writings conclude the volume.

⁓

**Harold Bloom** is Sterling Professor of the Humanities at Yale University and Henry W. and Albert A. Berg Professor of English at the New York University Graduate School. He is the author of over 20 books and the editor of more than 30 anthologies of literary criticism.

Professor Bloom's works include *Shelley's Mythmaking* (1959), *The Visionary Company* (1961), *Blake's Apocalypse* (1963), *Yeats* (1970), *A Map of Misreading* (1975), *Kabbalah and Criticism* (1975), and *Agon: Toward a Theory of Revisionism* (1982). *The Anxiety of Influence* (1973) sets forth Professor Bloom's provocative theory of the literary relationships between the great writers and their predecessors. His most recent books include *The American Religion* (1992), *The Western Canon* (1994), *Omens of Millennium: The Gnosis of Angels, Dreams, and Resurrection* (1996), and *Shakespeare: The Invention of the Human* (1998).

Professor Bloom earned his Ph.D. from Yale University in 1955 and has served on the Yale faculty since then. He is a 1985 MacArthur Foundation Award recipient and served as the Charles Eliot Norton Professor of Poetry at Harvard University in 1987-88. He is currently the editor of other Chelsea House series in literary criticism, including BLOOM'S NOTES, BLOOM'S MAJOR POETS, MAJOR LITERARY CHARACTERS, MODERN CRITICAL VIEWS, MODERN CRITICAL INTERPRETATIONS, and WOMEN WRITERS OF ENGLISH AND THEIR WORKS.

# Editor's Note

My Introduction meditates upon a moral tension between Joyce's psychological naturalism and use of a Dantean symbolism in "The Dead."

The Critical Extracts are fairly copious, so I will indicate here only what I judge to be a few high points. Patrick Parrinder usefully reminds us that Joyce's symbolism is only one of the modes employed in *Dubliners*, while Cleanth Brooks chooses "The Boarding House" as an exemplary story.

"Ivy Day in the Committee Room," one of Joyce's masterpieces, receives very informed commentaries from Joseph Blotner, Father S. J. Boyle, and Matthew Hodgart.

Lionel Trilling memorably ascribes something of our general sense of death-in-life to Joyce's "The Dead," after which Craig Hansen Werner traces a pattern in Gabriel Conroy's failures of sympathetic imagination in regard to women.

# Introduction

HAROLD BLOOM

It is an accurate critical commonplace to observe that Joyce's *Dubliners* is a vision of judgment, both Dantesque and Blakean. "The Dead," masterpiece of the volume, is overtly Dantean in design, as Mary Reynolds first demonstrated. In the final cantos of the *Inferno*, we are surrounded by the frozen wastes of Cocytus, where those are buried who have betrayed country, relatives, friends, benefactors, and guests. Gabriel Conroy, protagonist of "The Dead," evidently was viewed by Joyce as such a betrayer, though in thought and emotion rather than in his actions. Joyce's implicit judgment may seem rather harsh, but then Dante was perhaps the fiercest of all poetic moralists. Gabriel Conroy is weak and parasitical, a kind of failed artist, yet most of us would not regard him as damned. But we are not Joyce, or Dante, or Blake, or Milton, and all four seers—despite their differences—would have judged many among us as being already in Hell.

Poor Gabriel has some very humane qualities, which he shares with Joyce himself, and it may be, as many critics have maintained, that the anti-hero of "The Dead" is both a Joycean self-portrait and a self-condemnation, though that is too simple to be adequate for this ambiguous and exquisite novella. I have never believed in what Sir William Empson called "the Kenner Smear," that being the Eliotic attempt by Hugh Kenner to return Joyce to the Catholic orthodoxy against which the author of *Dubliners* was in rebellion. Original depravity is no more a Joycean idea than it was Blakean. When Gabriel Conroy passes a Last Judgment upon himself, we need not agree with its severity:

> A shameful consciousness of his own person assailed him. He saw himself as a ludicrous figure, acting as a pennyboy for his aunts, a nervous well-meaning sentimentalist, orating to vulgarians and idealizing his own clownish lusts, the pitiable fatuous fellow he had caught a glimpse of in the mirror.

There is something universal in that self-estimate; enough so to make many readers wince and grimace in recognition. Yet Joyce was gentler than Dante, and the creator of Poldy Bloom, the Ulysses of

Dublin, was no more a dark moralist than the benign Poldy proved to be. Sublimely, Poldy was a man without hatred, curious and gentle in all things. Gabriel Conroy is no Poldy, but neither is he a resident of Dante's Inferno, whatever Joyce's symbolic design. In *Ulysses*, the symbolic and naturalistic elements in Joyce's art fuse, but in *Dubliners* they tend to pull apart. Poor Gabriel's treasons are mundane enough; they are petty, as he so frequently can be petty. Perhaps he cannot get beyond self-love, and yet the great vision that concludes "The Dead" argues for a momentary self-transcendence:

> His soul had approached that region where dwell the vast hosts of the dead. He was conscious of, but could not apprehend, their wayward and flickering existence. His own identity was fading out. . . . ❀

# Biography of
# James Joyce

## (1882–1941)

James Augustine Joyce was born on the second of February 1882, in Dublin, Ireland, and was the oldest son of John Stanislaus Joyce, a tax collector, and Mary Jane Murray Joyce. During his childhood, the fortunes of the Joyce family deteriorated severely. To complicate matters, his father was known as a spendthrift and an alcoholic. Joyce attended Jesuit schools on scholarships. He attended Clonglowes Wood College from 1888 until 1893, when he was sent to Belvedere College and remained there until 1898. Then he enrolled in University College, Dublin. Joyce's first publication, entitled "Ibsen's New Drama," appeared in the April 1, 1900, issue of the *Fortnightly Review*. In 1902, Joyce received a degree in modern languages from University College, Dublin. After graduation he left for Paris, France, and planned to study medicine.

The years from 1902 to 1904 were troubled for Joyce but during this time he wrote the poems for *Chamber Music*. Joyce met Nora Barnacle in 1904, the year after his mother died. They met in June and in October they left Dublin to live on the Continent. The date for the action in Joyce's novel *Ulysses*, June 16, 1904, commemorates their first meeting. After leaving Dublin, Joyce and Barnacle settled in Trieste, Italy, where Joyce found a teaching position at the Berlitz School. Their first child, Giorgio, was born in Trieste in July of 1905. After a short stay in Rome in 1906, the family returned to Trieste. His daughter, Lucia, was born there in July of 1907.

In 1909, Joyce visited Ireland twice and opened the Volta Cinema in Dublin during his second trip. The Volta failed the next year. In 1912, Joyce brought his family with him on what would be his last visit to Ireland. In this year, Joyce wrote "Gas from a Burner" as a denouncement after the printer, John Falconer, destroyed the proofs of *Dubliners*. By a ruse, Joyce fortunately was able to save one copy of his collection of short stories.

During the next five years, Joyce was able to bring much of his work to light. In 1914, *The Egoist* began to serialize *A Portrait of the*

*Artist as a Young Man*, the result of his revision of *Stephen Hero*, Joyce's autobiographical text. The series continued through 1915. At the same time, Joyce began work on *Ulysses* and *Exiles*. By 1915, because of concerns brought on by World War I, Joyce moved his family to Switzerland. He also completed *Exiles*. *A Portrait of the Artist as a Young Man* was published in 1916. Then, in 1918, *Ulysses* began its serialization in *Little Review* (through 1920), the same year that *Exiles* was published. *The Egoist* started to publish installments of *Ulysses* in 1919.

In October of that year, Joyce returned briefly with his family to Trieste, but in 1920 he moved his family to Paris on the advice of Ezra Pound. At the same time, *Little Review* was ordered to stop its serialization of *Ulysses*. The first American controversy surrounding Joyce's major work occurred later in 1922. After Shakespeare and Company in Paris published *Ulysses* that year, the United States Post Office destroyed copies of it on its arrival. With its publication, Joyce gained much celebrity. He soon began work on *Finnegans Wake*. Between 1924 and 1927, Joyce published fragments of *Work in Progress* and then, in 1928, he published *Work in Progress Volume I* to protect his copyrights. By 1929, *Ulysses* had been translated to French.

The next years included a series of family-related events. Joyce had several eye operations, but never received medical attention for an undiagnosed ulcer. He married Nora in London on July 4, 1931. Then, in December of that year, his father died. In 1932, his grandson, Stephen James Joyce, was born. His daughter, Lucia, unfortunately suffered a mental breakdown around the same time.

When, in 1933, Judge John M. Woolsey of the U.S. District Court in New York ruled that *Ulysses* was not pornographic, the way was opened for Random House to publish the first edition of *Ulysses* in the United States in 1934. Two years later, the first British edition appeared. Then, in 1939, Joyce published *Finnegans Wake*.

In 1940 Joyce again found it necessary to move his family, this time because of the onset of World War II. Joyce, Nora, and Giorgio moved back to Zurich but had to leave Lucia in a mental hospital in France. Suffering from a perforated ulcer, Joyce was hospitalized in Zurich. Joyce died as a result of surgery on the ulcer on January 13, 1941. Nora, who survived him by ten years, buried Joyce in Fluntern Cemetery in Zurich. ❁

# Plot Summary of
## "The Sisters"

This story opens *Dubliners* and is the first that deals with childhood. Joyce first published the story in August of 1904 in an issue of the *Irish Homestead* under the pseudonym he used at the time, Stephen Daedalus.

The young narrator begins his tale with a note of doom. He reflects on Father James Flynn's hopeless condition, the result of a third stroke. The narrator sets this tone by remembering how, from the street, he checked the lights in the curate's windows. These hadn't changed so the young boy assumed that Father Flynn was still alive. He reflected: "Every night as I gazed up at the window I said softly to myself the word *paralysis*. It had always sounded strangely in my ears like the word *gnomon* in the Euclid and the word *simony* in the catechism. But now it sounded to me like the name of some maleficent and sinful being. It filled me with fear and yet I longed to be nearer to it and to look upon its deadly work."

But on returning to his aunt and uncle's house where he lived, the boy found them talking with Old Cotter, a tiresome neighbor whom the boy didn't like. Cotter was there to inform them of Father Flynn's death. At the news, the young narrator feigned disinterest as he ate. The older people continued to discuss the priest. His uncle explained that the boy had spent considerable time with Father Flynn. This provoked commentary from both the uncle and Cotter. They both agreed that an old priest was not the best company for a young boy.

> —What I mean is, said old Cotter, it's bad for children. My idea is: let a young lad run about and play with young lads of his own age and not be. . . . Am I right, Jack?

> —That's my principle, too, said my uncle. Let him learn to box his corner. That's what I'm always saying to that rosicrucian there: take exercise.

The narrator quietly objected to being called a child. Later, as he tried to fall asleep, the priest's gray face came to mind. The boy thought the face, strangely smiling, wanted to confess something to him and be absolved of sin.

The next day, the narrator went to the priest's house on Great Britain Street. It was part of a shop where umbrellas were repaired. The shutters were up and a crape bouquet adorned the door. On the bouquet a card announcing Father Flynn's death confirmed Cotter's news of the previous evening. The young boy thought of what he would have done if the priest had not really been dead. He would have found Father Flynn in his chair and would have fixed his snuff for him as usual. The boy remembered that the priest's hands shook so much that the snuff often spilled, so much so over the years that the priest's garments showed signs of fading where the grains of snuff had fallen.

The boy could not muster the courage to enter the house. Instead, he reflected on all that the priest had taught him. The priest, as his uncle had commented the night before, had explained history as well as the intricacies of the church to him. Father Flynn often asked questions to hear the boy's interpretation of certain sins. "His questions showed me how complex and mysterious were certain institutions of the church which I had always regarded as the simplest acts. The duties of the priest towards the eucharist and towards the secrecy of the confessional seemed so grave to me that I wondered how anybody had ever found in himself the courage to undertake them: and I was not surprised when he told me that the fathers of the church had written books as thick as the post office directory and as closely printed as the law notices in the newspaper elucidating all these intricate questions." After these questions, the priest would sometimes have the narrator recite the responses of the Mass.

That evening the aunt took her young nephew to pay their respects to Father Flynn's two sisters, Nannie and Eliza. Nannie received them in the hallway and led them into the bedroom where Father Flynn "had been coffined." The three knelt to pray but the narrator, lost in thought, paid more attention to Nannie's unevenly hooked skirt and her worn cloth boots. He thought that the priest would be smiling at such a sight. "But no. When we rose and went up to the head of the bed I saw that he was not smiling. There he lay, solemn and copious, vested as for the altar, his large hands loosely retaining a chalice. His face was very truculent, grey and massive, with black cavernous nostrils and circled by a scanty white fur."

Downstairs, they found Eliza seated in Father Flynn's chair. The young narrator went to his usual spot in the corner while Nannie occupied herself with getting the sherry and cakes for her company. As was to be expected in the circumstances, the aunt and Eliza talked about the deceased cleric. Eliza explained that Father Flynn died a peaceful death, having received the last rites of the Church. She agreed that he had been quite resigned:

> —That's what the woman we had in to wash him said. She said he just looked as if he was asleep, he looked that peaceful and resigned. No-one would think he'd make such a beautiful corpse.

Eliza also remarked that Father O'Rourke had made the arrangements after the death, bringing flowers and candlesticks from the chapel, writing the death notice, and seeing to the cemetery and the insurance. As she talked, Eliza realized that she would no longer have to bring in Father Flynn's tea, that he indeed was dead. The exchange of information turned slowly to more emotional thoughts as moments of silence marked the increasing difficulty bought on by remembrances. Eliza paused after she recalled Father Flynn's promise to take his sisters for a drive before the summer ended.

Then the conversation between the aunt and Eliza touched even closer to Father Flynn's problems. Another silence took over. In half-finished sentences, Eliza revealed two uncomfortable events in Father Flynn's final days. Eliza mentioned a broken chalice "that affected his mind." Later, when the parishioners, needing Father Flynn to go on a call, could not locate him, they finally found him sitting in the confessional laughing to himself.

Another silence reminded the narrator again of Father Flynn's dead body in the coffin. His tale ends as he recalled Eliza saying:

> —Wideawake and laughing-like to himself. . . . So then of course when they saw that that made them think that there was something gone wrong with him. . . . ❀

# List of Characters in
## "The Sisters"

*The narrator:* A young unnamed boy who has spent considerable time with the old priest, Father Flynn. The boy recalls his time with the priest as he deals with the news of the curate's death. He sees and senses a particular perspective of death while the adults around him focus on the priest's troubled later years.

*Father James Flynn:* An unkempt old priest, partial to snuff, has died, having suffering a third stroke. Though he tutored the young narrator in the intricacies of Church doctrine, all, except the boy, believed that the priest has lost his faith. He lived with two sisters, Nannie and Eliza, who, after his death, must contend with the reality of their loss and with the embarrassment caused by their brother's unconventional behavior.

*Old Cotter:* This is an old and tiresome neighbor who brings the news of Father Flynn's death to the narrator's aunt and uncle. Cotter expresses his negative opinions openly about the priest as he and the boy's relatives discuss the priest's death.

*Aunt and uncle of the narrator:* These are the young narrator's care givers. The uncle shares Cotter's opinion that an old priest is not the best companion for a young boy. The aunt brings her nephew to Father Flynn's home to pay their respects and to talk with the priest's sisters.

*Nannie:* Father Flynn's sister meets the narrator and his aunt at the door. She prays with them at the foot of the bed where Father Flynn lies dead. Her worn clothes catch the attention of the boy as they pray. Instead of talking with the aunt, Nannie occupies herself by serving cake and sherry.

*Eliza:* Father Flynn's other sister now sits in his old chair. She and the aunt talk about her brother. As their conversation progresses, Eliza remembers more and becomes troubled by her memories of a brother all considered to be conflicted. As she speaks, silence and pauses punctuate her speech and draw attention to the dilemma she faces. ❈

# Critical Views on
## "The Sisters"

[Joseph Chadwick has published articles on Sterne, Cortázar, and Yeats. Here, in his essay on the first short story in *Dubliners,* Chadwick maintains that the narrative silences in "The Sisters" protect the narrator not only from his elders but from the reader as well. In this extract, Chadwick attributes eucharistic qualities to the young narrator's words. Because of what Chadwick identifies as a transubstantiation, the boy endows his narrative with an authority apart from that he experiences in the real world.]

At one point in *Stephen Hero,* the narrator tells us that Stephen Dedalus

> spent days and nights hammering noisily as he built a house of silence for himself wherein he might await his Eucharist, days and nights gathering the first fruits and every peace-offering and heaping them upon his altar whereon he prayed clamorously the burning token of satisfaction might descend.

Stephen's first fruits and peace-offerings are the words he finds not only in Skeat's *Etymological Dictionary,* but also "in the shops, on advertisements, in the mouths of the plodding public." He, like the narrator of "The Sisters" with his word *paralysis,* builds a "house of silence" in which he can defend the words he collects from the depredations perpetrated upon them by their unwitting speakers. And he, again like that narrator, awaits the descent of "the burning token of satisfaction" which, Eucharist-like, will transubstantiate his words, make them flesh. Such transubstantiation, as both Stephen and the narrator of "The Sisters" seem to know (and if they, certainly Joyce too), is an appropriate ambition for a literary character. For only through such a process can a character in a book begin to acquire the status of a human being.

Silence's role in this transubstantiation consists in endowing the character and his word with their own authority and in defending them against the seemingly authoritative voices of other characters and of the reader. In "The Sisters," the narrator and his word gain their authority through the intimacy of their contact with silence and by transforming that silence into a positive power through which a recognition can be registered. But this transubstantiation can only work if we, as readers, can be made to forget the noisy hammering that goes into building the house of silence, and the clamorous praying that goes on inside it—if we can be made to forget, that is, that the house if silence is itself built of and inhabited by words. "The Sisters," unlike *Ulysses* and *Finnegans Wake*, seems to encourage such a forgetting; it seems to display at least some degree of faith in the power of the word to make us forget that it is a word, even if this power can only operate in a dream-like vision.

Even in "The Sisters," however, we can see the seeds of doubt about this power that come to fruition in the later works. One of these seeds is the very silence of God that seems to cause Flynn's spiritual malady. For if God is silent, no word can be made flesh. The pseudo-Eucharistic images that pervade the boy's encounters with the priest—the "packet of *High Toast*" snuff [my emphasis] the boy often brought Flynn and the sherry and cream crackers offered during his aunt and Eliza's conversation—imply, through their ironic deflation of the rite, that the chances for any kind of transubstantiation in this story are slender. The boy even refuses the cream crackers "because I thought I would make too much noise eating them," as if to suggest that partaking fully of this "communion" would somehow violate his understanding of the power of God's silence in Flynn's life, a power reaffirmed by the priest's silence in death. Another such seed of doubt is the echo of the story's first phrase—a thought of the narrator's—that we hear in its very last—a speech of Eliza's. This echo suggests that not even the words of the devotee of the house of silence can claim the transubstantiative power of the voice of God, that the devotee's words and those of the "plodding public" are not, finally, so very different:

> [Narrator:]
> There was no hope for him. . . .

> [Eliza:]
> there was something gone wrong with him. . . .

> —Joseph Chadwick, "Silence in 'The Sisters.'" *James Joyce Quarterly* 21 (Spring 1984): pp. 245–257. ✐

## Susan Swartzlander on Archaeological References in "The Sisters"

[Susan Swartzlander has written numerous essays on Joyce, Shaw, Hawthorne, and Faulkner. In this extract, ancient Egypt is the point of contact for an analysis of archeological references in Joyce's story, where Swartzlander finds echoes of a German novel by the same name, written by Georg Ebers.]

For [Georg] Ebers, as for Joyce, the mythological elements yield to the fresh-and-blood people who suffer the effects of a "creed outworn," a religion that rings hollow for its time and its people, entrapping, victimizing, and paralyzing. In both the short story and the novel, religion has become a theatrical show, emphasizing the superficial, the appearance over substance. In Ebers's *The Sisters*, the high-priest of the temple installs a device at the altar to ensure a fine "performance": the priest explains that "Any temple servant, hidden here behind the altar, can now light or extinguish the lamps without the illusion being detected by the sharpest." The high-priest tests the device, crying in a chanting voice: "Thus he commands the night, and it becomes day, and the extinguished taper, and lo! it flames with brightness. If indeed thou art nigh, oh, Serapis! manifest thyself to us." At these words a bright stream of light flashed from "the holy of holies," and again was suddenly extinguished when the high-priest sang: "Thus showest thou theyself as light to the children of truth, but dost punish with darkness the children of lies." The priest insists that such trickery is not deception: "We only present to short-sighted mortals the creative power of the divinity in a form perceptible and intelligible to their senses."

Joyce saw such an emphasis on matters of form in a Greek mass he attended, an observation he linked to his own short story:

> While I was attending the Greek mass here last Sunday it seemed to me that my story *The Sisters* was rather remarkable. The Greek mass is strange. The altar is not visible but at times the priest opens the gates and shows himself. He opens and shuts them about six times. For the Gospel he comes out of a side gate and comes down into the chapel and reads out of a book. For the elevation he does the same. At the end when he has blessed the people he shuts the gates: a boy comes running down the side of the Chapel with a large tray full of little lumps of bread. The priest comes after him and distributes the

lumps to scrambling believers. Damn droll! The Greek priest has been taking a great eyeful out of me: two haruspices.

In Joyce's "The Sisters," religion also assumes an air of theatricality. When he first thinks about visiting the deceased priest, as he is just about to recall his ecclesiastical lessons, the boy engages in "reading all the theatrical advertisements in the shop-windows." He then recounts Flynn's lessons about "the meaning of the different ceremonies of the Mass and of the different vestments worn by the priest." Flynn creates the same effect in the boy that Ebers's high-priest aims for, a sense of unquestioning awe: "His questions showed me how complex and mysterious were certain institutions of the Church which I had always regarded as the simplest acts." The boy wonders "how anybody had ever found in himself the courage to undertake" such "grave" duties as the Eucharist and Confession. The youngster is "put. . . through the responses of the Mass" and contemplates the fact that the Church fathers had written books as thick as the *Post Office Directory* and as closely printed as the law notices in the newspaper, elucidating all of these intricate questions."

Ebers and Joyce both describe institutions that bear the mark of simony, as it is defined most broadly, the prostitution of spiritual values. In both texts, simony carries with it the echoes of Simon Magus who used sorcery, theatre, to bewitch the people (Acts 8:9–24). In short story and novel, the authors expose religious institutions as not only deceptive but also as imprisoning forces that threaten individual freedom.

—Susan Swartzlander, "James Joyce's 'The Sisters': Chalices and Umbrellas, Ptolemaic Memphis and Victorian Dublin." *Studies in Short Fiction* 32 (Summer 1995): pp. 295–306.

## DONALD T. TORCHIANA ON THE CHARACTERIZATION OF FATHER FLYNN

[Donald Torchiana, Professor of English from Northwestern University, analyzes in this chapter of his book four words from "The Sisters": *gnomon, simony,* and *rosicrucian* from the final version, and *Providence* from the Irish Homestead

version. In this excerpt, Torchiana draws on Father Rosycross, the Masons, and Yeats to consider *gnomon* and *simony*
in particular as he interprets the characterization of Father
Flynn in the story.]

The blazing light of the priest's death-room, so reminiscent of the
light his followers discovered surrounding Father Rosycross's tomb
and unaltered body, may also mark the boy as his successor or one of
the illuminati-to-be. Moreover, he has his bread, so to speak, the world
of daily experience he is released into by the priest's death; perhaps
that is why Joyce has him sip wine only—a reminder of the Most Precious Blood and the quest he will inherit. Perhaps, too, Joyce's original
choice of St. Ita's Church for Father Flynn was based on the legend of
the saint's being discovered as a child in a blaze of light.

In keeping with this Masonic overlay with Rosicrucianism, especially as Father Flynn resembles the figure in Yeats's essay, consider
the second term, *gnomon*, notably as it occurs in the boy's Euclid.
Instead of the parallelogram with a similar parallelogram removed
from it and, by extension, any such incomplete figure, we discover
that even more primary meanings attach to the word: "a thing
enabling something to be known," and then the "term used of a
mechanical instrument for drawing right angles"—a carpenter's
square. Such a square is a prime symbol of craft masonry (quite visible on the Masonic Hall in Molesworth Street, close to the National
Library), the insignia for a Master Mason and a symbol of the great
allegory of Masonry, the legend of the Master Builder, Hiram Abiff.
In this sense, Father Flynn is also a kind of master builder—and the
title from Ibsen's play may also be echoed—and mentor for the boy,
the future literary craftsman.

In the same manner, the word *simony* is related to both *Rosicrucian* and *gnomon*, for a high grade among Rosicrucians—who originally aimed at purifying the Catholic church—has the title Magus.
For Father Flynn to be called a simoniac, then, may merely be for
him to resemble Simon Magus, who also learned his magic, it is said,
in Egypt. Among the legends clinging to his name, one is particularly
apt for Joyce's purposes. It finds him disputing his divinity with
Peter and Paul before the Emperor Nero. In an effort to prove his
powers, Simon Magus then attempted to fly but fell to his death,
surely a Daedalian theme dear to Joyce. One recalls that Stephen's
father in both the *Portrait* and *Ulysses* is named Simon. Nor is such a

fall without its imaginative appeal to a student of Ibsen's *Master Builder* like Joyce. Those, then, who exonerate Father Flynn from any act of simony may well be right. He has nevertheless assumed the magical role of Simon Magus in furthering the literary bent of a boy who will someday contend with Peter and Paul before a new Roman Authority, and finally take it upon himself to fly to preserve his artistic integrity, or call it his literary magic.

—Donald T. Torchiana, " 'The Sisters': The Three Fates and the Opening in *Dubliners*" in *Backgrounds for Joyce's "Dubliner."* (Boston: Allen & Unwin, 1986): pp. 18–35.

# Plot Summary of
## "Araby"

The story concentrates on childhood, the first of the thematic divisions in *Dubliners*. It was written in October of 1905, but not published until 1914.

The young narrator describes his street as quiet and conscious of the decent lives therein, disturbed only when the Christian Brothers' School lets out its students each day. In his house, a priest had died in the back drawing room. He had been a tenant of the family and had left several books that the narrator enjoyed perusing. There was a garden, in the back of the house, which had been let go wild where an apple tree and some bushes still could be seen.

Along with a description of his street, the young boy explained the activities that occupied him and his companions. In winter, it was dusk before they finished dinner. Their play outside was in the increasing darkness of the night spotted only by the faint light of the street lanterns. The boys ran and played until their bodies no longer noted the winter's cold. If they saw the narrator's uncle returning home, they would hide. If Mangan's sister came to the door to call her brother to tea, the narrator would, from a safe distance, watch the movements of her dress and hair.

Each morning the young boy waited for the first sight of Mangan's sister. As soon as he saw her, he would grab his schoolbooks and walk after her, passing her eventually on the way. He never spoke to her on these morning treks. No matter where he went, the image of Mangan's sister accompanied the young narrator. Whether helping his aunt with the groceries or during prayers the young boy thought of her. "I thought little of the future. I did not know whether I would ever speak to her or not or, if I spoke to her, how I could tell her of my confused adoration. But my body was like a harp and her words and gestures were like fingers running upon the wires."

When, at last, she spoke to him, the boy did not know how to answer. Mangan's sister asked if he was going to Araby, the bazaar. She said that she would love to go, but couldn't because her convent-school had scheduled a retreat for the same time. As she spoke, the narrator noticed how the door lamp lit up the curve of her neck and shone on her hair. The light fell so that he could see the border of her petticoat. Finally as if wakening, he promised to bring her something from the bazaar.

That night the young boy could think of nothing else except the vision of Mangan's sister. He asked his aunt for permissions to go to Araby on Saturday night. Then, on Saturday morning, he reminded his uncle of the bazaar. But when his uncle had not yet returned home at dinnertime, the boy became irritated. In the meantime, he put up with hearing the cries of his friends from the street and the gossip of old Mrs. Mercer at his aunt's table.

Finally, at nine o'clock the uncle came home. The boy's aunt reminded her husband that the boy had been waiting for his uncle to give him some pocket money for the bazaar. After what seemed to the boy a series of endless delays, he arrived at the magical site at ten minutes to ten. In his haste, he could not find the cheap entrance and so paid the highest fee to enter. He noticed from the silence upon entering the bazaar that only a few stalls were still open.

Remembering his original purpose, the boy approached a stall where a woman was talking with two young men. The young boy noticed their English accents and listened to their vacuous conversation. At last, the woman obligingly interrupted her chat to attend to the boy. But he could not focus on the articles for sale. As she turned back to continue talking with the young men, the narrator realized that the bazaar was closing and that the place was almost completely dark. His excursion ended as he reflected: "Gazing up into the darkness I saw myself as a creature driven and derided by vanity: and my eyes burned with anguish and anger." ❀

# List of Characters in
## "Araby"

*The narrator:* A young boy who lives and plays on a typical street soon becomes obsessed by the vision of his friend's sister. He follows her and daydreams about her, but he cannot work up the courage to speak to her. When she finally talks to him, the young narrator promises to bring her something from the magical bazaar called Araby. Both the girl and the bazaar are the boy's center of attention. His goal is compromised when he must wait for his uncle's return.

*Mangan's sister:* A girl who has no first name, this is the neighbor of the young narrator. The sweep of her dress and her hair fascinate the boy. He follows her as she walks to her convent-school. He watches as the light of a door lamp falls on her neck and reveals her petticoat. When Mangan's sister talks to the narrator, she tells him of her desire to go to Araby. He makes both the girl and her wish his mission in life.

*Aunt and uncle of the narrator:* The care givers of the young narrator, the aunt gives him permission to go to the bazaar, but the uncle comes home so late that the boy arrives at the bazaar only a few minutes before it closes. ❀

# Critical Views on
## "Araby"

ZACK BOWEN ON METAPHORS IN "ARABY"

[Author of several studies on Joyce and on Irish literature, Zack Bowen concentrates on everyday happenings such as inclement weather in conjunction with allusions to the old priest and sexual images in this extract. Bowen contends that the booth at the Araby bazaar serves as a "metaphor of a debased confessional" by which the young narrator learns that his quest is futile.]

In the last of the bildungsroman trilogy, "Araby," we are again reminded of Flynn's death: "The former tenant of our house, a priest, had died in the back drawing-room." Lest we forget that the priest's death had sexual overtones and was linked with exposure, we are also informed that "The wild garden behind the house contained a central apple-tree and a few straggling bushes under one of which I found the late tenant's rusty bicycle-pump." The apple-tree-knowledge metaphor, combined with the priest's rusty bicycle pump—rusty presumably from exposure—certainly appear to have typically Joycean double meanings. When in the next sentence we learn that the priest left his furniture to his sister, the association with Flynn is complete.

The boy's incantation to Mangan's sister is linked directly to inclement weather, the priest, and sexual imagery:

> One evening I went into the back drawing-room in which the priest had died. It was a dark rainy evening and there was no sound in the house. Through one of the broken panes I heard *the rain impinge upon the earth, the fine incessant needles of water playing in the sodden beds* [emphasis added]. Some distant lamp or lighted window gleamed below me. I was thankful that I could see so little. All my senses seemed to desire to veil themselves and, feeling that I was about to slip from them, I pressed the palms of my hands together until they trembled, murmuring: *O love! O love!* many times.

The rain impinging upon the earth and the water coming down in needles playing in sodden beds link inclement weather with the sexual metaphor. Though the passage has overtones of Blessed Virgin Mary adoration, it is also highly sexually charged. The boy's final epiphany at the bazaar is about his own vulnerability and foolishness. The conversation between the female attendant and her two young gentlemen is a coarse parody of his conversation and relationship with Mangan's sister:

—O, I never said such a thing!

—O, but you did!

—O, but I didn't!

—Didn't she say that?

—Yes, I heard her.

—O, there's a . . . fib!

The boy comes to a realization of the futility of his own romanticized quest through the metaphor of a debased confessional. At the end of the story the preponderance of ecclesiastical allusions, the emptied church, the salver, etc., heightens the correspondence of the early part of the story with its religious counterpart in "The Sisters," and again teaches the narrator-protagonist a lesson about exposure. This time that exposure involves his emotions and how he has, not unlike Stephen Dedalus, created an artifice of chivalric adherence to a courtly love code to justify his own adolescent sexual behavior. In this case the cloak to ward off exposure was, like its successor in *A Portrait,* the creation of an artistic mythos, but through its final analogy to the banalities of everyday life, it is routed and epiphanized.

—Zack Bowen, "Joyce's Prophylactic Paralysis: Exposure in *"Dubliners." James Joyce Quarterly* 19 (Spring 1982): pp. 257–74.

## BEN COLLINS ON MANGAN'S SISTER AS THE FOCUS OF "ARABY"

[In this excerpt, Ben Collins, author of several essays on Joyce, identifies Mangan's sister as the focus point of the story. Collins emphasizes that she has no first name and suggests a relationship to the Irish poet James Clarence

Mangan. Further, Collins connects the boy's quest and its chalice to other *Dubliners* texts.]

But it is to Mangan's sister that we must turn to find the focal image of the story. She is, after all, the object of the boy's affection, and like him she is purposefully unnamed. Through her Joyce can sum up and indicate the true breadth of the moral paralysis. She represents Church (in that she includes Christ, Mary, and the priesthood), Ireland, and the betrayer Judas.

That she is *Mangan's* sister, that she has no other name than Mangan, forces the reader to dwell upon that name. Those informed will be minded of the Irish poet James Clarence Mangan, said to be an inspiration to the Irish movement but nevertheless admired by Joyce and the subject of an early essay by him in St. Stephen's. To the world, Mangan is known, if at all, for his "The Dark Rosaleen," a translation and adaptation of an old Irish poem. Though seemingly a poem of love, the work is an allegory in which a hero (Hugh the Red O'Donnell) is coming to save Ireland (the Dark Rosaleen) from the Saxons (the English) who are besetting her. The men of God (Church and Pope) are also on their way with help and gifts to raise Ireland from her inglorious position. By allusion to this poem, the themes of love and religion are re-enforced and the theme of nationality—about which Joyce has already concerned himself by mention of the come-all-you's of O'Donovan Rossa and the ballads about the troubles of the country—is introduced. Modern Ireland is in a like situation, beset by England and in need of a hero. The role of Mangan's sister as deity is made known, if it cannot establish itself in any other way, comically, for one little knows Joyce who feels that he was unaware of or incapable of using Mangan's initials—J.C.

But mere allusion in this case is not enough; there must be comment, however recondite. In his hopeless love for Mangan's sister, the boy reverts to his experiences of the two earlier stories, bringing into play the idea of *quest* and the *chalice*. His love intensifies the illusion that the world has romantic and religious content, and he can go through the sordid streets bearing, but not dropping, his imaginary grail. He is the knight errant, the courtly lover, coursing through throngs of imaginary foes in places "hostile to romance"—where patriotic songs are sung—as well as Mariolater where the "shrill litanies of shopboys" are heard and whence "her name sprang to my lips at moments in strange prayers and praises which I myself did not understand."

—Ben L. Collins, " 'Araby' and the 'Extended Simile' " in *Twentieth Century Interpretations of "Dubliners."* Ed. Peter K. Garrett (Englewood Cliffs, N.J.: Prentice-Hall, Inc., 1968): pp. 93–99.

## Garry M. Leonard on the Magical Bazaar

[In this detailed study, Garry Leonard rereads *Dubliners* from a Lacanian point of view. Here, in this extract, Professor Leonard focuses on the tram ride that the young narrator takes to Araby, the magical place that represents for the boy the culmination of his quest. Leonard maintains, based on Lacanian principles, that the trip to such a place depicts a shift in control from the boy to the object of his desire, Mangan's sister.]

In traveling to the Araby Bazaar, the boy boards a special train. People press against the doors in an attempt to enter, but they are pushed back and told that it is "a special train for the bazaar." For the entire trip past "ruinous houses," the boy remains "alone in the bare carriage." At the end of the ride, the uniqueness of his journey persists as he steps out of the train on to "an improvised wooden platform" just recently constructed. Standing alone on the deserted platform, he sees in front of him "a large building which displayed the magical name." All these details suggest that the boy sees his journey as traveling to someplace other than Dublin. It is different from anywhere; it is magical. The boy's fantastic hope for the place gives it a fairy tale quality. The tawdry building seems enchanted to him only because of an enormous act of faith on his part. Its status as magical is as tenuous as the fantastic unity of his subjective consciousness. The magical power of symbolization begins when a child realizes something is missing. The power of language to evoke what is not present depends on the feeling that something is lacking. His later realization that the bazaar is a commercial sham, perpetrated on the naive for profit, will destroy the place as symbol but will have no effect on the powerful dynamic of symbolization. The narrator experiences his sexual awakening as the advent of unity, whereas Joyce's story of the presence of Mangan's sister outside the confines of the boy's narrative gives an opposite account of sexuality based solely on its divisions (division of the subject, division between subjects). It is her representation in the boy's narrative as the Woman and her absence from it as a woman that makes his story of himself possible. "Araby" is not about the loss or gain of this or that object, it is about the impossible structure of desire for both the masculine and feminine subjects.

The boy on the improvised platform sees displayed before him what is described as "the magical name" rather than the word "Araby." Like Mangan's sister, the bazaar implies something beyond what can be named or represented. What the narrator hopes he will see is the world before it has been crossed through by the word. The actual bazaar is irrelevant; in his own mind, he has traveled beyond time and space to the land of the Other, authorized to do so by a woman who, as The Woman, represents this land. This magical name does not exist anymore than she does. He hopes to discover the lost object that would end the primacy of the signifier over his subjectivity. He presumes she must desire this most precious of all signifiers because it was her appearance to him as lack—as feminine—that convinced him of the existence of a Holy Grail that could authenticate who he is. The magical bazaar could return him to the imaginary pristine duality of the mirror stage before he seized the false scepter of language and began to rule a world within the world where words are always ruling him (the boy, like Martha Clifford in *Ulysses*, does not like "that other world").

The Araby Bazaar is magical for the boy because he believes it will be a place beyond mere representation where the lost object he needs to complete himself will be found. This object is not hidden in a geometrical or an anatomical space; if that were so, he would have found it long ago. It is not hidden at all; it is always elsewhere "in" a symbolic structure that can only be perceived in its effect. In taking upon himself her pilgrimage, he is inevitably drawn into becoming the object of her desire, even as he tries to make her subject to his desire.

—Garry M. Leonard, "The Question and the Quest: The Story of Mangan's Sister" in *Reading "Dubliners" Again: A Lacanian Perspective* (Syracuse: Syracuse University Press, 1993): pp. 73–94.

[Author of *Joyce's Web: The Social Unraveling of Modernism*, Professor Norris treats the concept of "blind" in terms of the street on which the narrator lives, his point of voyeurism, and his own emotional blindness. In particular, Norris suggests in this excerpt that the hunter's blind from which the boy observes Mangan's sister can be taken as a Lacanian scotoma.]

The story's solipsism and insularity is figured by the opening topography of North Richmond Street as "blind," as a cul de sac and dead end from which escape is baffled. The slippage of meaning that leads that figure of the "blind" from spatial to ocular closure, links the street, and its houses with their virtual hermetic seals, to the larger thematics of closed economies in which exchange, and communication, is doomed to recirculation. The boy's house—while not clearly identical with the uninhabited house at the end of the blind street—is figured as an enclosure of negativity, of death, waste rooms, waste papers, waste people and waste lives. The sealed rooms—"musty from having been long enclosed"—circulate as little air as the rusty bicycle pump abandoned in the garden. They in turn mirror that figure of closed economy: Mrs. Mercer, the pawnbroker's widow, who extends her late husband's business of recycling used goods to her philanthropy ("collected used stamps for some pious purpose"), and to her communication ("I had to endure the gossip"). Herself constructed like a closed system, Mrs. Mercer, not surprisingly, feels herself endangered by fresh air ("the night air was bad for her"). The story's allusions to baffled pneumatic circulation itself circulates verbal bafflements, like an impaired pentecostal pneuma or wind, from other *Dubliners* stories ("one of them new-fangled carriages . . . them with the rheumatic wheels").

The slippage of "blind" continues to recirculate through the narration's topological system. The narration describes the boy's voyeurism of Mangan's sister by slipping further meaning off the protective screen that is called a "blind," onto its meaning as an ocular shelter used by hunters to conceal or camouflage them from their prey ("The blind was pulled down . . . so that I could not be seen"). This figurative transformation of the boy's house into a version of a duck or deer 'blind' is quite congruent with the boy's subsequent activity of essentially 'stalking' the girl, who is described as a "brown figure," a deer (or dear):

Every morning I lay on the floor in the front parlour watching her door. The blind was pulled down to within an inch of the sash so that I could not be seen. When she came out on the doorstep my heart leaped. I ran to the hall, seized my books and followed her. I kept her brown figure always in my eye and, when we came near the point at which our ways diverged, I quickened my pace and passed her.

Visually, the boy's voyeurism enacts a curious visual encapsulation that we might miss were it not for the introductory image of the 'seeing' houses. The nearly closed blind, with its slit for peeping, functions like an eyelid closed but for a slit—transforming the front parlor into an eye that harbors the peeping boy. The boy's own ocular gesture—"I kept her brown figure always in my eye"—is thus doubled, as the 'seeing' house keeps the boy in its eye. This strange figuration has complex ontological implications since an eye cannot see itself (except as mirrored or reflected, that is, as some other eye would see it). The boy in his hunter's "blind" thus looks out from a blind spot, what Jacques Lacan has termed a "scotoma." The implication of the boy doing his seeing from the site of his blind spot, is that he cannot see himself, cannot see himself as a voyeur or a stalker, for example, since he sees himself only as a worshiper or a lover.

—Margot Norris, "Blind Streets and Seeing Houses: Araby's Dim Glass Revisited" *Studies in Short Fiction* 32 (Summer 1995): pp. 309–318.

## Donald T. Torchiana on the Rite of Passage in "Araby"

[In this section of Professor Torchiana's study of *Dubliners*, he focuses on the young boy's rite of initiation as symbolized by entering Araby, the magical bazaar where he seeks a gift for Mangan's sister. Torchiana points out that the boy finds himself caught between two worlds, a realization that provokes anger and anguish.]

While many a critic has discovered elements of the grail quest in the boy's visit to Araby—and I would suggest the Irish legend of the Cauldron of Dagda as equally pertinent—the actual initiation has remained a troublesome point. Yet the boy has come seeking a gift. He has entered a hall described as resembling a church after the service; up to this point he has been inwardly blind. He appears to enter the stall only to examine the wares. He must in fact walk alone and need go no further. The jars at the darkened entrance to the stall resemble Eastern guards. That is enough. The growing darkness around him is really a kind of light. Gate, Central Hall, and Eastern stall have brought him to a discovery of himself. And his aunt had hoped that the bazaar wouldn't be "some Freemason affair."

How does he discover himself—that is the natural question. Perhaps a key sentence is the one following "At the door of the stall a young lady was talking and laughing with two young gentlemen." It reads: "I remarked their English accents and listened vaguely to their conversation." I take it that "their" in both cases refers to the "two young gentlemen," for the makeup of the bazaar, as I have shown, was overwhelmingly Irish, while the possibility of two English visitors at the end of Whit week for the last night of Araby was most likely. In other words, an Irish girl (called a "young lady" four times), probably Catholic if she merely tends the stall before closing on the last night, is making up to two young Englishmen. All seem older and socially superior to the boy. The second question to be asked is what is the conversation about, the subject of the story's epiphany? It sounds like a promise, or the hint of a promise, real or imaginary, which she would or would not deny—not a lie but a fib, perhaps no more than [sheer] banter yet also something very much like the romantic illusion of a charity bazaar where Irish maidenhood has a chance to display its beauty under the aegis of the Lord-Lieutenant. The boy was vain to think otherwise. Not unlike the priest of the first story, his chalice has been broken. But, instead of laughing in the dark, he very nearly weeps. His anguish and his anger define his dilemma: anguish that he must return empty-handed, anger for idealizing what has turned out to be a trivial flirtation, a mockery of his own idealized lust. Like most double agents, he is caught between both sides.

—Donald T. Torchiana, " 'Araby': The Self-Discovery of a Double Agent" in *Backgrounds for Joyce's "Dubliners"* (Boston: Allen & Unwin, 1986): pp. 52–67.

# Plot Summary of
## "The Boarding House"

This is the last of four stories in *Dubliners* that focus on adolescence. Joyce finished the story in July of 1905, but it was not published until it appeared in *Dubliners* in 1914.

A capable woman, Mrs. Mooney was the daughter of a butcher and was married to her father's foreman. Together they opened a butcher shop near Spring Gardens. Her husband's behavior, though, changed radically after his father-in-law died. Not only did he drink heavily, but he also took money from their accounts. When Mr. Mooney began to buy bad meat for the shop, their business went to ruins. After he tried to attack Mrs. Mooney one night with a meat cleaver, she petitioned the Church for a separation, retaining the custody of her children, Jack and Polly.

Mrs. Mooney left her husband without home or means of support "and so he was obliged to enlist himself as a sheriff's man. He was a shabby stooped little drunkard with a white face and a white moustache and white eyebrows, pencilled above his little eyes, which were pinkveined and raw; and all day long he sat in the bailiffs' room, waiting to be put on a job." On the contrary, Mrs. Mooney made a successful transition. She used the little money that remained from the butcher shop to start a boarding house on Hardwicke Street. The all-male clientele was made up of two groups of residents: tourists or *artistes* from the music halls, and clerks who worked in the city. All the residents call this imposing and firm woman The Madam. The young men staying at the boarding house paid the same rate and shared in the same interests.

Jack, Mrs. Mooney's son, was a clerk in town. The residents knew him to use obscenities and to come home in the wee hours of the morning. He always had a joke to tell and always knew where the action was. On Sunday nights, the residents would gather in Mrs. Mooney's drawing room. Jack and the others would sing songs and share stories, especially when the *artistes* were present.

Polly, The Madam's 19-year-old daughter, who had light hair and green-gray eyes, would also join in the singing. For example, one night she sang:

*I'm a . . . naughty girl.*
*You needn't sham:*
*You know I am.*

Mrs. Mooney had intended for Polly to work as a typist but when her father began stopping by her place of work to visit his daughter, Mrs. Mooney took her home and made her do the housework.

The residents enjoyed Polly's presence in the house and Polly reciprocated by flirting with them. Mrs. Mooney kept a watchful eye and her distance since most of the flirtations were harmless. Then, sometime later, she realized that Polly and one particular young man shared more than just a passing interest. Mrs. Mooney waited and watched until she finally and firmly took action. "She dealt with moral problems as a cleaver deals with meat: and in this case she had made up her mind."

On an early summer Sunday morning, the open windows of the boarding house let in the beckoning sound of the nearby church bells. Mrs. Mooney sat and watched her servant, Mary, clear the breakfast dishes. As Mary cleaned up and put everything away, The Madam mentally reviewed the talk she had had with Polly the night before. Both women had been frank during the conversation and Mrs. Mooney's suspicions had been confirmed.

It was then that Mrs. Mooney noticed that the clock said seventeen minutes past eleven. She knew that she had enough time to speak to the boarder, Mr. Bob Doran, and to leave before twelve o'clock as she had planned. Mrs. Mooney also knew that she had the upper hand. Society was on her side and since Mr. Doran was around 35 years old, he could not make any excuses of ignorance or youth to defend his actions. Mrs. Mooney instead concentrated on the reparation that Mr. Doran should make. When she thought she had considered all the possibilities, Mrs. Mooney sent Mary for Mr. Doran. She had figured that he would not risk his job and life because of any bad publicity. She concluded that marriage was the only option. At half-past eleven, The Madam stood up to check herself in the mirror before the confrontation.

Meanwhile, Mr. Doran was already quite nervous that Sunday. As he tried to shave, Doran recalled how badly his session had gone in the confessional the night before. The priest had emphasized the gravity of his sin and had given him two alternatives: marriage or flight. First Doran considered what his employer would do if the scandal became public knowledge. But then Doran's thoughts turned to marriage. The problem, according to Doran, was Polly and her family. Her father's reputation and her mother's boarding house were not the best recommendations for a young woman. Doran thought for a moment that he was being trapped.

He remembered clearly when the relationship changed from chaste caresses to something more serious. Doran was reminded of Polly coming to his room one night, then he thought of her nearness as he ate his dinner each evening and of the pleasures of her company. But when those pleasures eventually subsided, Doran didn't know what the future would hold. At this moment, he heard Mary's summons.

As Doran descended the staircase, his glasses fogged up. He stood a moment to clean them. As he did, the images of The Madam and his employer loomed heavily over Doran's thoughts. Jack Mooney passed him on the stairs at this moment. Doran was reminded of an evening in the drawing room. Jack had become so violent when an *artiste* made a comment about Polly that everyone else tried to subdue him. Doran then recalled the threat Jack had made: "The musichall *artiste*, a little paler than usual, kept smiling and saying that there was no harm meant but Jack kept shouting at him that if any fellow tried that sort of a game on with *his* sister he'd bloody well put his teeth down his throat, so he would."

At the same time, Polly was in her room crying. After she washed her face and rearranged her hair, she sat back on her bed and suddenly felt almost cheerful. Her thoughts occupied her mind such that Polly no longer saw the pillows on her bed nor did she remember why she was waiting there. This all changed when she heard her mother speak:

—Come down, dear. Mr Doran wants to speak to you. ✷

# List of Characters in
## "The Boarding House"

*Mrs. Mooney:* After a violent outburst by her husband, Mrs. Mooney takes her children, Jack and Polly, and leaves him homeless. She uses some family money to start a boarding house where clerks from the city and tourists from Liverpool stay. Mrs. Mooney is a clever and imposing woman whom the residents call The Madam. By careful reflection and characteristic cunning, she takes control of a very delicate situation when her daughter's flirtations with a boarder cause embarrassment for all involved.

*Mr. Mooney:* He married the daughter of his employer, but when his father-in-law died, Mr. Mooney changed radically. He took money from the family business, bought bad meat for the butcher shop, and suffered from a reputation of being a drunkard.

*Jack Mooney:* Among the boarders at his mother's house, Jack was known to use profane language and to stay out until the early hours of the morning. He could tell a good joke and always knew where to find diversion.

*Polly Mooney:* She was originally sent to work as a typist but when her father began to visit her, Mrs. Mooney insisted that Polly stay home to do the housework. The Madam's 19-year-old daughter often flirted with the residents of her mother's boarding house. One day, however, Mrs. Mooney realized that the flirting had gone too far.

*Mr. Bob Doran:* This 35-year-old clerk boarded at Mrs. Mooney's house like others clerks in the city. When his relationship with Polly took a more compromising turn, Mrs. Mooney intervened. Doran felt pressure, implied as well as direct, to pay for his actions. ❀

# Critical Views on
## "The Boarding House"

CLEANTH BROOKS ON THE CRAFT OF "THE BOARDING HOUSE"

[The renowned scholar and critic Cleanth Brooks chose "The Boarding House" when asked to write on a perfectly crafted short story. In this extract, Brooks mentions other equally fine short fiction by writers such as Hemingway and Welty and then explains his choice of Joyce's tale.]

*Dubliners* is a remarkable book. But one is by no means confined to it if he is choosing an instance of the perfectly crafted short story. There are many more to be found: the very best of Hemingway, for example, or something as quietly beautiful as Eudora Welty's "A Piece of News." Yet if one is asked for a specimen of a quite perfect short story, one which makes its point convincingly and which is so carefully organized that it could hardly lose one word without real loss to its quality, and yet a story which needs not a single word more to produce its effect, "The Boarding House" constitutes an excellent choice.

The little story goes about its business immediately, directly, and almost bluntly. It tells us that its principal character, Mrs. Mooney, was a butcher's daughter, and if this little unadorned statement sets the tone for what is to follow, it also acquires more and more meaning as Mrs. Mooney's story develops. For example, it helps explain why she married her father's foreman and set up a butcher shop of her own. But the marriage clearly was not made in heaven: her husband drank heavily, plundered the till, fought with his wife, and after the night in which he went for his wife with a butcher's cleaver, Mrs. Mooney managed to get a formal separation. She used what was left of her money to set up a boarding house.

This is, I suppose, necessary exposition, but it is lively writing, nevertheless. We learn a good deal, not only from the facts related but from the deft dispatch with which they are delivered. The storyteller obviously knows Mrs. Mooney, though he is not particularly fond of her, and he gets quickly on through little more than a summary of earlier events to what he regards as a story worth his telling.

—Cleanth Brooks, "James Joyce's 'The Boarding House.'" *Studies in Short Fiction* 25 (Fall 1988): pp. 405–8.

## GARRY M. LEONARD ON CONVERSATIONS AND BOB DORAN

[The author of many articles on Joyce, Professor Leonard concentrates on the Lacanian concept of remembered speech as he examines the text depicting the character of Bob Doran. Professor Leonard draws attention to the scarcity of actual dialogue or action in this part of the story and suggests that, in this way, Joyce highlights Doran's subjectivity by recreating the voices of others in his consciousness.]

Throughout this story, it is the context in which a conversation is conducted that is presented to the reader, not the actual words that are exchanged. Other interviews that are presented by Joyce as a sort of psychological dumb show include the one in which Mrs. Mooney confronts her daughter, the one in which she confronts Bob Doran, and the one in which Bob Doran proposes to Polly (having barely survived an interview with his priest the night before, which also is not recounted to readers). One can add to this all the several possible interviews that Bob Doran imagines he now will have to endure because "something has gone on" between Polly and him. There is, first of all, Mr. Leonard, his boss at the great Catholic wine merchant's office where he has worked for thirteen years: "He felt his heart leap warmly in his throat as he heard in his excited imagination old Mr. Leonard calling out in his rasping voice: *Send Mr. Doran here, please.*" Here, finally, is a bit of direct dialogue, but it is from an interview that has not yet occurred! Another bit of direct dialogue plays in Doran's mind as he "hears" the talk of his friends: "He could imagine his friends talking of the affair and laughing." Doran "hears" this direct dialogue through the perspective of his laughing friends, and then he "hears" Polly speaking in the manner that will provoke such talk: "She was a little vulgar, sometimes she said *I seen* and *If I had've known*." Even the phrase that periodically distinguishes itself in his mind from the competing noise of all the other phrases is not original to him: "He echoed her phrase, applying it to himself: *What am I to do?*" One final piece of dialogue—Jack's vow that "if any fellow tried that sort of a game on with *his* sister he'd bloody well put his teeth down his throat, so he would"—filters through Doran's mind. Joyce's use of italics makes it clear that Doran's consciousness exists against a background of static, with an occasional phrase tuning in to give the effect of subjectivity; as soon as Mrs. Mooney figures out the various wavelengths he operates within, it is a simple matter for her to push his buttons. Looking over this list, it seems fair to say that Doran's "self" consists of conversations he has had, conversations he has overheard, and conversations he hopes to avoid. He seems a particularly apt example of Lacan's point that consciousness is a constellation of remembered speech that is undermined by speech that has been forgotten. In short, Doran's subjectivity is presented by Joyce as a cacophony of shouting and accusing voices, none of them his, yet all of them intermingling to form the broadcast of himself.

By the time Doran puts on his coat and waist coat to go to his interview with Mrs. Mooney ("more helpless than ever"), he has the motion of a reluctant robot powered by the dynamic of all the voices in his head: "A force pushed him downstairs step by step. The implacable faces of his employer and of the Madam stared upon his discomfiture." The fragmented discourse going through his head suggests that what he takes to be his personality is actually what he imagines other people see when they speak of him or to him. Of Jack Mooney's vow to protect his sister's virtue, he simply assumes he is the implied audience. Mrs. Mooney and Mr. Leonard represent all the people who Bob Doran has imagined confirming who he takes himself to be. That is, they occupy the space of the Other through which Bob Doran constitutes the structure of his subjectivity. For Lacan, the subject is one who must interview someone else, an other, to center his identity in a reality generated by language. Language constitutes people as a subject, and, thus, the difference between "self" and society is only an imaginary distinction that protects people from the realization that they are not distinct entities, but signifiers who act as signifiers of other signifiers (other subjects).

—Garry M. Leonard, "Ejaculations and Silence: Sex and the Symbolic Order in 'The Boarding House' " in *Reading "Dubliners" Again: A Lacanian Perspective* (Syracuse: Syracuse University Press, 1993): pp. 132–48.

## Donald T. Torchiana on Polly as Madonna

[Professor of English at Northwestern University, Donald Torchiana concentrates in this extract on Polly and the dramatic shift of attention to her in the final page of the story. Torchiana considers this final scene a "very human version of the Annunciation" and suggests a relationship between Polly and the virgin birth.]

On that barely single page of conclusion, following the first true page break in the story, all our attention is fixed on Polly. As all readers of the story know, Joyce had described her earlier as "a little perverse madonna." Her "wise innocence" is also a sly version of Christ's urging his disciples to be "wise as serpents and innocent as doves." On the other hand, Doran himself may resemble Joseph in his justness, his kindliness, basic celibacy, thoughtfulness when he discovers Polly's condition, even in his wish to spare her disgrace, though we must not forget his early wish like Joseph's to put her aside. Both men are known for their attention to religious duty. Both are relegated to family life. Both were sober, industrious workers, given the exception of Doran's later annual benders. To be sure, this comparison has elements of the wildest blasphemy in it. Yet so does much more in the story—even Polly's lighting her candle at his, suggesting that lighting a paschal candle might be something like Tenebrae for Doran. Still, this last page belongs to the pregnant Polly.

Having dried her eyes and refreshed them with water, she sits at the foot of the bed, contemplates the pillows, and falls into a reverie. Thereupon she is filled with "hopes and visions," this last phrase repeated: "Her hopes and visions were so intricate that she no longer saw the white pillows on which her gaze was fixed or remembered that she was waiting for anything." What were these hopes and visions? At the risk of being called an academic Christologist, I would venture that Joyce is quietly presenting a very human version of the Annunciation, feather pillows and all, in its total calming joy. Polly cannot be called full of grace. She is not blessed among women, though she *will* be married. For the moment, amazingly enough, she is transported beyond the pillows before her and beyond the exigencies of her troubling pregnancy. Her visions and hopes, transport and trance beyond seeing and remembering, may well be delusions. But Joyce delicately hints that she shares them in common with at least one other *enceinte* Mary and her supposedly celibate spouse.

The teasing unlikelihood of such a virgin birth and its veneration in Dublin faintly colors the entire story. Most particularly it mocks Mrs. Mooney's haste in going about her business of reparation with Doran. At 11:17 A.M. the Madam drifts into a reverie in her chair, recounting her advantages in the brief exchange to ensue. At nearly 11:30 she dispatches the servant Mary to fetch Doran. Her hope is to make short twelve at Marlborough Street, that is, low mass at St. Mary's Pro-Cathedral at twelve noon, celebrated at the side altar.

—Donald T. Torchiana, " 'The Boarding House': The Sacrament of Marriage, the Annunciation, and The Bells of St. George's" in *Backgrounds for Joyce's "Dubliners"* (Boston: Allen & Unwin, 1986): pp. 109–124.

## Fritz Senn on Wrong Turnings in "The Boarding House"

[Author of a collection of essays on Joyce entitled *Joyce's Dislocations: Essays on Reading as Translation,* Fritz Senn discusses "The Boarding House" in terms of a love story gone wrong. Joyce, according to Senn, leaves the reader out of the main events and thus constructs a context of wrong turns and misdirections. In this way, like Polly and Mr. Doran, the reader is left to be manipulated by Mrs. Mooney's forces.]

The following views are offered as supplementary angles from which we might profitably talk about Joyce's "The Boarding House." Some of its features are those of a love story; we find all the conventional trappings: a young girl and a not so young man; they are brought together by circumstance and opportunity; there is the promise of a marriage in the near future, except that things are not quite as they ought to be; things are out of place. The ruling passion is practically absent, and what is present seems to be awry. The couple, it takes little imagination to discern, is mismatched, united by direct and implicit forces and by scheming. What is in evidence is the trapping. "The Boarding House" gains much of its poignancy by being set off against a backdrop of sweep, comforting fiction of the "Matchem's Masterstroke" type. It is a love story of wrong turnings.

Its misdirection involves readers by leaving them largely out of the main events. We realize how we are cut off from the crucial events, both of them; we are detained by moments in between; the actions are off stage. We are never informed what actually happened between Mr. Doran and Polly Mooney. We learn about the enticing beginning of the affair but not its completion. We may guess, of course, and we may think we know enough. Still, the overall narrative agency and all three main characters are in harmonious collusion in withholding the facts from us. We are not even told anything concrete about the interview between mother and daughter of the night before in which, we read, "a clean breast" had been made "of it"; nor about Mr. Doran's confession. Nothing specific is passed on to us. Whenever we come close to that recent "sin" as the cause of it all, the narrative drifts into vagueness, generalities, "his delirium . . . " or "secret amiable memories . . . a revery"; we are not let into the secret of "every ridiculous detail." The ellipsis after "delirium," Joyce's, needs to be filled, and filled it will be, by a few readers with more certainty than the facts may warrant. The sin is one for which "only one reparation" can be made (there is tacit agreement on this between Mrs. Mooney and Mr. Doran's priest, who both use the word independently, which in turn tells us that the case is a standard one, not unique), but still small enough to allow of being "magnified" by a priest. The one chief witness and victim remembers an exchange of "reluctant good-nights" on the third landing. All things known considered, Mr. Doran might have to pay for much less than what we almost automatically charge him with: this would make the reparation more cruel, less contingent on deed than on mere social attitudes, "honour," or reputation, hearsay and gossip. Anyway, we were not there, and this gap is paralleled by the one in the present, the decisive interview when Mrs. Mooney will be "hav[ing] the matter out with Mr. Doran." There is no need for us to be on the spot (nor is Polly's presence required). The issue has been predetermined by a determined woman in full charge, and by Mr. Doran's known "discomfiture." Like a general before a battle, Mrs. Mooney has marshalled her forces, her arguments, even their phrasing. We may well stay with Polly and the vaguest of her memories, waiting, alone. We can fill *this* narrative vacuum easily, though we were somewhere else, apart.

—Fritz Senn, " 'The Boarding House' Seen as a Tale of Misdirection" in *James Joyce's "Dubliners."* Ed. Harold Bloom (New York: Chelsea House Publishers, 1988): pp. 121–129.

# Plot Summary of
## "Ivy Day in the Committee Room"

This story in *Dubliners* centers on public life. It was completed in the summer of 1905 and then published in 1914.

The tale begins as Old Jack carefully stirred the cinders and then fanned the coals in the chilly room. His old and bony face showed moist blue eyes that blinked at the fire he tended. As he rose, he addressed a gray-haired, pockmarked young man named Mr. O'Connor. The young man slowly rolled some tobacco, licked the paper to form a cigarette, and then asked Old Jack when Mr. Richard Tierney would return. Old Jack did not know and he went to get a match for the young man. Instead of waiting, O'Connor pulled out of his pocket a business card, announcing Mr. Tierney's campaign, and used part of it to light his cigarette.

It was a cold and rainy sixth of October. Both men now shared the Committee Room on Wicklow Street: Old Jack because he was the caretaker, and O'Connor since the bad weather interrupted his canvassing efforts on Mr. Tierney's behalf. Old Jack picked up a previous conversation to complain about his 19-year-old son's bad habits. As he and O'Connor exchanged opinions on how to straighten out Old Jack's son, another man, Mr. Joe Hynes, came in from the rain. Mr. Hynes was tall and thin, a young man with a light brown moustache. He greeted O'Connor but as he did he also grumbled about the darkness of the room. Old Jack lit two candles, which completely changed the aspect of the surroundings.

Hynes asked if Tierney had paid O'Connor yet. When O'Connor answered no, Old Jack made a sharp comment that provoked a discussion among the men. They debated the honesty of the working-class candidate, Colgan, versus that of a "publican," Tierney. Directing himself to O'Connor, Hynes remarked:

> —One man is a plain honest man with no hunkersliding about him. He goes in to represent the labour class. This fellow you're working for only wants to get some job or other.

But he and Old Jack continued to spar verbally, while O'Connor thought only of collecting his pay. They all quarreled about the impending visit by the English King Edward and the expected welcoming speeches and then, "The three men fell silent. The old man began to rake more cinders together. Mr Hynes took off his hat, shook it and then turned down the collar of his coat, displaying, as he did so, an ivy leaf in the lapel."

—If this man was alive, he said, pointing to the leaf, we'd have no talk of an address of welcome.

Another silence followed, interrupted only by the arrival of a little man called Mr. Henchy. He talked to O'Connor about his canvassing that day. It was clear both men wanted to be paid. When Hynes referred to their candidate as Tricky Dicky Tierney, Henchy agreed.

—O, he's as tricky as they make 'em, said Mr Henchy. He hasn't got those little pig's eyes for nothing. Blast his soul! . . . Mean little shoeboy of hell!

Old Jack came into the room with more coal and Henchy and O'Connor talked on. Then Hynes said goodbye to all and left the room slowly; only O'Connor replied. After a few minutes, Henchy asked the two men what business brought Hynes to the Committee Room. Henchy offered the opinion that Hynes was in fact working for Colgan, in other words, he was spying for the opposition. Old Jack tended to agree but O'Connor defended Hynes. Just as Henchy implied that Hynes would sell his country, they heard a knock on the door and in walked a man looking like a priest.

Mr. Henchy was the first to recognize the man as Father Keon and bade him to come in. The priest explained that he was only looking for a Mr. Fanning who, according to Henchy, could be found at the Black Eagle. Henchy lit the way for Father Keon to the stairs. The others gossiped some about the priest and then turned their comments back to Tierney and political corruption in general. Another knock on the door interrupted them.

This time it was a delivery boy from the Black Eagle with the long-promised bottles of stout. Old Jack helped him to transfer the bottles to the table. Mr. Henchy sent the boy to borrow a corkscrew. When the boy returned, the men opened three bottles and offered another one to the boy. He happily accepted, drank up the contents, grabbed the borrowed corkscrew, and left with a polite word.

The three men enjoyed their stout as they continued their conversation. While Henchy reviewed his canvassing that day, two other men, Crofton and Lyons, came into the Committee Room. Henchy told Old

Jack to serve them some beer. When the caretaker reminded him that there was no corkscrew, Henchy took two bottles and put them near the fire. Crofton, originally a canvasser for the Conservative Party, had begun working for Tierney. As the men talked, the first cork popped out of the bottle set aside for Lyons.

The discussion turned to the upcoming speech by the King of England. Henchy voiced his support because he maintained that the speech would generate income for Ireland. O'Connor, however, wanted to mention Parnell but was cut off by Henchy. Lyons tried unsuccessfully to take over the flow of the conversation.

> —But after all now, said Mr Lyons argumentatively, King Edward's life, you know, is not the very. . . .
>
> —Let bygones be bygones, said Mr Henchy. I admire the man personally. He's just an ordinary knockabout like you and me. He's fond of his glass of grog and he's a bit of a rake, perhaps, and he's a good sportsman. Damn it, can't we Irish play fair?

When O'Connor managed to interject that it was Parnell's anniversary, the other cork exploded out of the stout bottle. At the same time, Joe Hynes came in and Old Jack placed another bottle by the fire for him.

Henchy, changing his tone, addressed Hynes and congratulated him for having remained loyal to Parnell. At that point, O'Connor asked Hynes to recite the poem he had written in Parnell's honor. After some hesitation, Hynes began:

> He is dead. Our Uncrowned King is dead.
> O, Erin, mourn with grief and woe
> For he lies dead whom the fell gang
> Of modern hypocrites laid low.
> . . . .
> The day that brings us Freedom's reign
> And on that day may Erin well
> Pledge in the cup she lifts to Joy
> One grief—the memory of Parnell.

A silence filled the room when Hynes finished and was followed by a hearty burst of applause. The cork burst out of the bottle set aside for him, but Hynes did not seem to hear it as he sat bareheaded and flushed. Mr. Henchy asked Crofton what he thought of the poem. "Mr Crofton said that it was a very fine piece of writing." ❈

# List of Characters in
## "Ivy Day in the Committee Room"

*Old Jack:* The caretaker of the Committee Room, Old Jack pays attention to the fire and interjects his opinion, when possible, in the conversation of the canvassers that gather there. Old Jack complains as well about the bad habits his young son exhibits.

*Mr. O'Connor:* A young canvasser who works for Mr. Richard Tierney's campaign by soliciting support in the neighborhood. O'Connor has come to the Committee Room because of the inclement weather. He waits and hopes that Tierney will pay him for his work.

*Mr. Richard Tierney:* A candidate in the municipal elections, Mr. Tierney never appears in the story but is often discussed by the men. They refer to him as Tricky Dicky Tierney. He came from a humble background but now seems to forget those who have helped him or worked for him.

*Mr. Joe Hynes:* A true supporter of the Irish hero Parnell, Hynes is suspected by Henchy of working for the opposition candidate, Colgan. He wears the ivy leaf in his label as a reminder of his loyalty to Parnell. Hynes recites his poem in honor of Parnell at the close of the story.

*Mr. Henchy:* A little man, Henchy supports the impending arrival of the English King Edward because he thinks the royal visit will bring money to Ireland. Henchy instigates and gossips throughout the many conversations in the story. He suspects Hynes of spying but then congratulates him for remaining loyal to the hero Parnell.

*Crofton* and *Lyons:* These are two other canvassers who come into the Committee Room to share stout and conversation with their colleagues. ❀

# Critical Views on
## "Ivy Day in the Committee Room"

JOSEPH BLOTNER ON CHRISTIAN OVERTONES IN "IVY DAY"

[In an analysis of the Christian overtones of this Dubliners story, Joseph Blotner also provides a clear explanation of the title. Ivy Day, the Committee Room, and the wearing of the ivy are described to support Professor Blotner's study of the Christian elements he observes in the tale.]

The locale of "Ivy Day in the Committee Room" is an upper room in a building in Dublin. The room's elevation is emphasized when Mr. Henchy grasps a candlestick at Father Keon's departure "to light him downstairs" because "'the stairs is so dark.'" This suggests the upper room which was the meeting place of the apostles in Jerusalem in which the Last Supper was held (Luke, 22:12) and in which the election of Matthias to fill the place of Judas took place (Acts, 1:13). It seems logical to assume that it was this same upper room in which the spirit of the Holy Ghost descended upon the apostles at Pentecost (Acts, 2:12). More important for purposes of this analysis, it can be assumed that it was probably this same upper room in which the risen Christ appeared to the apostles (John, 20: 19, 16).

Even the story's title is rich in allusion. Ivy Day is a commemoration of the death of Parnell, the lost leader. "Committee Room" here denotes the place in which the canvassers meet; but for these men and nearly all of Joyce's Irish readers, it would connote a vastly different place: Committee Room No. 15 in the House of Commons in London, where, after days of fierce recriminations, Parnell had been deposed from the leadership of the Irish parliamentary party following Gladstone's letter declaring that the Irish cause would be injured and his own position made untenable if Parnell retained his post. The starkness of the contrast is clear: on the one hand, a tense and crowded chamber in the seat of the oldest legislative body of the English-speaking peoples, where national issues and the fate of national figures hung upon the action; on the other hand, a cold and shabby room in an undistinguished section of Dublin, where nothing is accomplished politically, which is a genuine "centre of paralysis." The ivy, which is green and perennial, a symbol of life and rebirth, is worn here with a fundamentally ironic effect for a man who is dead, and with whose death had departed the fire and spirit which he had infused into the movement he led.

Interpreted still another way, the wearing of the ivy leads deeper into the symbolism of the story. Both O'Connor and Hynes wear the ivy leaf in their lapels. This marks them, just as the symbol of the fish marked the early Christians, signalling their commitment to a leader, an ideal, and a cause. For the Christians there was the hope of a resurrection that would make their symbol more than a memento. For a time, some of the Parnellites had cherished the same hope. "— Some say he is not in that grave at all," says John Power in awed tones in Ulysses, "That the coffin was filled with stones. That one day he will come again." But the same Hynes shakes his head, "—Parnell will never come again, he said. He's there, all that was mortal of him. Peace to his ashes."

—Joseph L. Blotner, " 'Ivy Day in the Committee Room': Death Without Resurrection" in *James Joyce's "Dubliners": A Critical Handbook*. Eds. James R. Baker and Thomas F. Staley (Belmont, Calif.: Wadsworth Publishing Company, Inc., 1969): pp. 139–146.

## JAMES FAIRHALL ON POLITICS AND THE STORY

[Professor Fairhall examines in this study the local election campaigns, particularly those of 1902 and 1903 that he believes Joyce used for this story. Here, in this extract, Fairhall explains how the character of Hynes is necessary to establish the presence and absence of Colgan in the story, which serve, in Fairhall's opinion, as metaphor for Dublin's poor and absent citizenry.]

Colgan, of course, exists only insofar as Hynes defends him against old Jack and makes a series of short, propagandistic comments to the effect that the workingman "gets all kicks and no halfpence" and "It's labour produces everything." The question must be asked: why do he and the entire working-class population of Dublin (save the compromised caretaker) remain offstage in this political story written by an increasingly radicalized socialist? One reason, perhaps, why Joyce chose not to portray them directly is that the unity of *Dubliners* depends in part on its focus on a single (though many-leveled) social class. Another reason may be that he was largely a stranger to the world of the Dublin masses and that he saw Dublin through middle-class eyes. Thus "Ivy Day" is first and foremost an expression of the bourgeois Parnellism that he inherited from his father and only secondarily a reflection of the social and socialist issues of turn-of-the-century Dublin politics. Ultimately, it could be pointed out, all of Joyce's fictional views of Dublin and Ireland are subject to a kind of ideological parallax, as a result of which the thing observed is modified by the observer's position in a certain social class and culture.

But Joyce was no ordinary observer. The silences and absences in his fiction resonate with what is left unsaid and what is missing and convey meanings that could hardly be conveyed otherwise. Socialism, the rights of labor, the living conditions of the urban poor—these were all repressed subjects within the ideology of middle-class Irish nationalism (no less so, after the Split, for the Parnellites than for their foes). Not that they were not discussed—they were, but always in terms of and within the context of the dominant ideology, with no true dialogue or engagement taking place. Joyce assigned to "Ivy Day," as one of the "stories of public life in Dublin" (*Letters II* 111), the topic of politics. Inevitably, given his deep-rooted Parnellism and the preeminence of the Nationalists who had claimed Parnell's mantle, he focused on the contrast between the great leader and his unworthy, venal, ineffectual successors. This contrast gradually comes to occupy the foreground of the story. Colgan and the one-third of Dublin's citizens who lived in the slums linger out of sight in the wings.

—James Fairhall, "Colgan-Connolly: Another Look at the Politics of 'Ivy Day in the Committee Room.'" *James Joyce Quarterly* 25 (Spring 1988): pp. 289–304.

## M. J. C. Hodgard on Charles Steward Parnell and "Ivy Day"

[M. J. C. Hodgard, author of *The Ballads and Song in the Works of James Joyce* (along with Mabel P. Worthington), explains the theme of Parnell in the story in this extract. Not only does Hodgart trace the appearance of Parnell in other Joycean texts but also he suggests a basis for Hynes's poem to Parnell as well. The verses, Hodgart contends, may have been conceived from a song composed by John Stanislaus Joyce in 1896.]

This is Joyce's most moving treatment of the theme of Parnell, who haunted him throughout his career. The theme can be followed through the Christmas dinner scene in the *Portrait*, the 'Aeolus', 'Hades', 'Oxen', and 'Eumaeus' chapters of *Ulysses* and in all parts of *Finnegans Wake*. Joyce early came to identify Parnell the Uncrowned King with Christ the King: each was delivered to his enemies by the treachery of his friends. In his article in the *Piccolo della Sera* of 16 May, 1912, 'L'Ombra di Parnell' (the 'shade' again suggests a ghost, as in Yeats's poem) he wrote of Parnell's melancholy conviction 'that in his hour of need, one of the disciples who dipped his hand in the same bowl with him would betray him . . . That he fought to the very end with this desolate certainty in mind is his greatest claim to nobility.' Joyce followed a current notion in identifying Parnell with Moses, the Leader who brought the children of Israel out of Egyptian bondage to within sight of the Promised Land; he develops this trope in 'Aeolus' and in 'The Oxen of the Sun', where Moses is a type of Christ, as in the Liturgy. The trope of the lost leader who will return from the tomb is developed in 'Hades' and further elaborated in *Finnegans Wake*, where Parnell is one of the types of the Phoenix. Joyce's identification of Stephen Dedalus as the Artist with Parnell ('indifferent, paring his fingernails') is well known. One must not suppose that the rich train of association (Parnell-Moses-Christ-Stephen) was in Joyce's mind when he wrote 'Ivy Day'; but the notions of Parnell as ruler ('the only man that could keep that bag of cats in order') and as the Lord betrayed 'to the rabble-rout of fawning priests' are central. . . .

Hynes' poem, which according to Ellmann may have been based on one called 'Erin's Heroes' composed by John Stanislaus Joyce and sung by him in 1896, is a masterpiece of bathos. It is a deadly parody of the sentimental patriotic rubbish typical of the Irish popular music of the previous century. Yet it not only conveys Hynes' genuine feelings, to which his audience cannot help responding, but also sums up the basic themes of the story: Christ, traitors, priests, and resurrection 'like the Phoenix from the flames'. Throughout the story the cold and damp of an October evening has been emphasized: the fire of life is almost out. 'Old Jack raked the cinders together'; O'Connor lights his feeble cigarette with an election card; there are only 'a few lumps of coal' for the fire and two candles. Everyone comes in cold, Mr. Henchy 'rubbing his hands as if he intended to produce a spark from them'. It is the fire kindled by Parnell in his heyday that has been quenched. '–Musha, God be with them times! said the old man. There was some life in it then.' The talk circles round bad fathers and errant sons: Parnell, unlike Old Jack, Larry Hynes, Victoria or Edward, was the just but stern father who alone could have kept Erin's children in order: '*Down, ye dogs!*' The characters, especially Mr. Henchy, present a microcosm of Irish treachery: each politely agrees with the other to his face, only to turn on him with wit and malice behind his back—a notable Irish trait observed by many besides Joyce. But through the absurdities of Hynes' poem there shines, obscurely but unwaveringly, an image of the heroic and lonely men who sacrificed themselves for the Irish cause, to bring about 'the dawning of the day'.

—M. J. C. Hodgard, "Ivy Day in the Committee Room" in *James Joyce's "Dubliners."* Ed. Clive Hart (London: Faber & Faber, 1969): pp. 115–121.

SYLVIA HUNTLEY HOROWITZ ON CHRISTIAN ALLEGORY IN THE STORY

[In this extract, Sylvia Huntley Horowitz associates the etymology of Joe Hynes's surname with Christian references. While, in her essay, Huntley Horowitz illustrates that Hynes can be considered either a Thomas or a Judas, here she assigns Christlike qualities of death and resurrection to Joe Hynes.]

The Irish surname, Hynes, derives from *eidhin*, meaning "ivy" (MacLysaght). The word sounds like the plural of "hind," which has two meanings: it is a farm laborer and a deer. If Joe Hynes just dropped in to sponge a drink, we have an image of a thirsty deer, an image that strongly suggests a thirsty soul, one who longs for God. "As the hind pants for the water brooks, so my soul pants after thee, O God." Finally, the English word "hyne" is defined in the OED, "From this world; out of this life (*Baith heir* and *hyne*, both in this world and the next)." Joe Hynes, like Christ, is not of this world (John 17:14).

During Joe's absence, in our allegory the time in the world between Christ's death and His resurrection, the population in the Community Room acknowledges or at least works for its shady trinity—Fanning, Cowley, Tierney—and tries out for fun another one, Henchy occupying the Mansion, with Old Jack as father, Keon as Holy Ghost, and Mat O'Connor as Moses or Matthew. The arrival of the dozen of stout is payment from Tierney in a form that makes all his canvassers feel more loyal, powerful, expansive, and generous. It restores their faith in worldly power and money. The conversation focuses on King Edward VII (an anti-Christ like Tierney, a charismatic leader whose coming will make a difference), and on Parnell. Parnell is dead, and his spirit—a yearning for freedom, for Irish independence, for equality—is really dead.

> —Our side of the house respects him because he was a gentleman.
>
> —Right you are, Crofton! said Mr. Henchy fiercely. He was the only man that could keep that bag of cats in order. *Down, ye dogs! Lie down, ye curs!* That's the way he treated them. Come in, Joe! Come in!

Henchy welcomes Joe because his own world is in order—the values are perfectly straight: money and power—and Joe is no threat because, after all, there was something great about old Parnell—he was a power. In Henchy's mind Joe is like one of the curs the old chief would have put down.

The resurrected Christ, Joe Hynes, is completely misunderstood, his poem a great success. "When it had ceased all the auditors drank from their bottles in silence." Hynes remains "sitting, flushed and bareheaded on the table." If he looks like a sacramental meal on the Lord's table, they won't partake of it, for they get their spirit elsewhere.

> —Sylvia Huntley Horowitz, "More Christian Allegory in 'Ivy Day in the Committee Room.'" *James Joyce Quarterly* 21 (Winter 1984): pp. 145–154. ℗

[In this study, Professor O'Grady examines the presence of
Charles Stewart Parnell in Joyce's text. In particular,
O'Grady focuses on the character of Hynes and his declara-
tion of allegiance to Parnell by reciting a poem in Parnell's
honor. The poem, as O'Grady points out, contains clear references to Ireland but also to a Judas image since the
betrayal of Parnell is carried out "with a kiss."]

The only self-redeeming character in the story is Joe Hynes. In contrast with O'Connor and all the others, he is, "a tall slender young
man"—young despite the fact that ten years have passed since Parnell's death, and Hynes had been a supporter even then, as Henchy
acknowledges: "There's one of them, anyhow, . . . that didn't renege
him." Now a supporter of Colgan, the Fenian candidate, Hynes
endorses the working-man, unlike Tierney and his followers, who
seek only personal gain:

> —The working-man, said Mr. Hynes, gets all kicks and no halfpence.
> But it's labour produces everything. The working-man is not looking
> for fat jobs for his sons and nephews and cousins. The working-man
> is not going to drag the honour of Dublin in the mud to please a
> German monarch.

But Hyne's most significant admission of his political stance is his
poem, "*The Death of Parnell:* 6th October, 1891." This poem, so typical of those published at the time of Parnell's death in such newspa-
pers as *United Ireland*, functions in several ways in the story. Not
only is it an accurate example of the popular literary treatment of
the Parnell story, but it also reflects on and illuminates the rest of
"Ivy Day in the Committee Room." As a part of the Parnellite literary
tradition, the poem contains references to "Our Uncrowned King";
to poetic "Erin"; to "coward hounds"; to Ireland's noble "statemen,
bards, and warriors" and to her "heroes of the past"; and, of course,
to the Phoenix. But hidden among these conventional phrases and
references are a number of subtle allusions to Hyne's audience: they
are clearly a "fell gang/Of modern hypocrites" with "coward caitiff
hands"; their potential for "treachery" is unquestionable; they, in
effect, "befoul and smear th' exalted name/Of one who spurned
them in his pride." The "fawning priests—no friends of his" are represented, of course, by Father Keon. And the references to the "pyre"

and to the Phoenix are obviously consistent with the symbolic significance of the atmosphere in the Committee Room.

But the image which best reflects Joyce's own attitude toward the betrayal of Parnell is that of betrayal "with a kiss." This Judas image is one which Joyce refers to ironically, in his essay "Home Rule Comes of Age," as Irish altruism: "They have given proof of their altruism only in 1891, when they sold their leader, Parnell, to the parasaical conscience of the English Dissenters without exacting the thirty pieces of silver." Henchy refers to Major Sirr in terms which echo Judas's betrayal of Christ; then Henchy himself is seen as a Judas willing to compromise, for "capital," the integrity of his country; and all except Hynes are in the Committee Room, ultimately, in the hopes of getting paid for canvassing for a political candidate whom they neither like nor trust.

The only verbal acknowledgment which Hynes's poem receives is from Crofton, the Conservative, who "said that it was a very fine piece of writing." Actually it is not; but it is sincere—the only sincere expression in this story of post-Parnell Ireland. But it is also with Hynes's sincerity that Joyce's "critical" view of history takes exception. Although for a purpose contrary to Lyons's, Hynes too "monumentalizes" Parnell—in this case as a model to emulate. In evoking Parnell, Hynes implies that "the great thing existed and was therefore possible, and so may be possible again."

—Thomas B. O'Grady, " 'Ivy Day in the Committee Room': The Use and Abuse of Parnell" in *James Joyce's "Dubliners."* Ed. Harold Bloom (New York: Chelsea House Publishers, 1988): pp. 131–141.

# Plot Summary of
## "Grace"

Joyce wrote this story in late 1905. It belongs to the division in *Dubliners* that focuses on religion and public life.

An unpleasant scene opens the first part of the story. Two men in the lavatory of a bar attempt to lift up a drunken man whom they find lying on the dirty floor. They bring him upstairs to the bar where the manager questions them about the man's identity. Seeing how gray the unconscious man's face is, the worried manager calls for a policeman. In the meantime, a ring of men already in the bar forms around the drunken man. The policeman arrives and begins interrogating the manager about the man. Then a cyclist made his way through the crowd and started to care for the injured man. He washed the blood from the man's mouth and asked for some brandy. The man opened his eyes finally after the brandy was forced down his throat.

The man got to his feet with some assistance and announced that he felt fine. The policeman started to question him but the unfortunate man did not pay any attention. A tall gentleman, Mr. Power, walked into the commotion and recognized the drunkard as Tom Kernan. The newcomer told the policeman that he would take charge of bringing Kernan home. Mr. Power asked Tom how he had come to be in such a state. The young cyclist interjected to explain that Tom had fallen down the stairs. Tom tried to thank him for his assistance but was unable to speak clearly. Once in a cab, Mr. Power leaned over to look more closely at Tom. He noticed the blood around his teeth and saw that a small part of his tongue seemed to have been bitten off in the fall. The two men headed toward Tom's home. Kernan was a teataster and salesman for a London tea company. Power was a younger man and worked in the Royal Irish Constabulary Office in Dublin. As Kernan's success declined, Mr. Power's had increased, but they had remained friends.

When they arrived at Kernan's home, Mr. Power turned Kernan over to his wife, who helped her husband to bed as she had done on many other occasions. Then, when Mr. Power and Mrs. Kernan talked, Power made a point of explaining that he had walked in on the unfortunate scene. He sympathized with Mrs. Kernan and consoled her as he could. Power promised that he would consult his other friend, Martin Cunningham, about Kernan's troubles, and together they would "make a new man of him."

In the central part of the story, Tom's friends, having advised Mrs. Kernan of their plans, come to visit him at home with the intention of persuading him to attend a spiritual retreat with them. Mrs. Kernan, a practical woman who had learned to cope with the difficulties that twenty-five years of marriage to Kernan represented, managed her household as well as possible. She had two sons who already were employed and on their own. The other younger children were left to be educated despite the worries brought on by their father. "There were worse husbands."

Two nights after the unfortunate incident, Kernan's three friends, Martin Cunningham, Mr. M'Coy, and Mr. Power, came to the house to visit him. The three good Catholics were determined to bring Kernan back into the fold. Kernan was from a Protestant family but had converted to Catholicism when he married. He had not fully participated in church activities for at least twenty years. On the other hand, Cunningham, an older colleague of Power's, knew the benefits of the church. Everyone knew that Cunningham's wife was an incurable alcoholic. Cunningham, sympathized for his marital problems, was known to be sensible, influential, and intelligent. Mrs. Kernan accepted their plan. "Religion for her was a habit and she suspected that a man of her husband's age would not change greatly before death. . . . However Mr Cunningham was a capable man and religion was religion. The scheme might do good and, at least, it could do no harm."

The men talked about Kernan's accident. M'Coy, who had once been a tenor and was now the secretary to the City Coroner, asked with some interest about the pain caused by Kernan's injuries. Cunningham and M'Coy emphasized that Kernan's discomfort was really a result of the alcohol in his system. Kernan did not have to give them too many details about the men with whom he had been drinking. He mentioned Harford's name and without saying much more, because of Harford's reputation, the men could imagine what had transpired. Kernan thanked Power for helping him out of a delicate situation with the policeman. It was then that the men subtly introduced the idea of the retreat.

—O, it's nothing, said Mr Cunningham. It's only a little matter that we're arranging about for Thursday.

—The opera, is it? said Mr Kernan.

—No, no, said Mr Cunningham in an evasive tone, it's just a little . . . spiritual matter. . . .

—To tell you the truth, Tom, we're going to make a retreat.

—Yes, that's it, said Mr Cunningham, Jack and I and M'Coy here—we're all going to wash the pot.

Cunningham feigned surprise and suggested that Kernan join them "to wash the pot." Kernan remained silent while the others talked about the Jesuits.

There was general agreement that the Jesuits were among the most capable clerics in the church. Kernan listened most to Cunningham's opinions and finally asked him for more information about the retreat. As if to persuade him more, Cunningham told Kernan that Father Purdon was holding the retreat for businessmen. The men discussed Father Purdon, but Kernan preferred to mention Father Tom Burke who, according to Kernan, had always attracted large crowds of both Catholics and Protestants to his sermons. As they talked, Mrs. Kernan came in to announce the arrival of Mr. Fogarty, the grocer.

A man of good manners with the housewives who frequented his store, Fogarty showed a certain amount of grace in his movements. He came bearing a half-pint of whiskey for Kernan. Glasses were made available and the whiskey was shared. Cunningham brought the conversation back to the topic of the popes and Pope Leo XIII in particular. The three men bound for the retreat discussed Pope Leo and his work and in general tried to keep Kernan's attention on track. Cunningham related the story of two cardinals who doubted the infallibility of the pope. The German cardinal ended up leaving the church, but the other, John MacHale, submitted once he heard the pope speak. "Mr Cunningham's words had built up the vast image of the Church in the minds of his hearers. His deep raucous voice had thrilled them as it uttered the word of belief and submission." As Mrs. Kernan came in, Power addressed her:

—Well, Mrs Kernan, we're going to make your man here a good holy pious and God-fearing Roman Catholic.

He swept his arm round the company inclusively.

—We're all going to make a retreat together and confess our sins—and God knows we want it badly.

—I don't mind, said Mr Kernan, smiling a little nervously.

Kernan agreed to the retreat but refused any part of holding or lighting candles once there.

The final part of the story describes the retreat briefly and focuses on Father Purdon's sermon. Many gentlemen had already filled most of the Jesuit church when Kernan and his friends arrived. M'Coy tried to make some funny remarks as the men tried to find a place to sit together. Many familiar faces were in the crowd. Cunningham made a point of showing Kernan that Harford, the moneylender who accompanied him in his drunken escapade, was already seated in one of the pews. Finally they noticed the arrival of Father Purdon, his "massive red face appearing above the balustrade."

Father Purdon quoted the passage about the "Mammon of iniquity" as the basis of his sermon. He appealed to them as businessmen and professionals. "If he might use the metaphor, he said, he was their spiritual accountant and he wished each and every one of his hearers to open his books, the books of his spiritual life, and see if they tallied accurately with conscience." Father Purdon ended his sermon by asking the men to set their accounts right. ❁

# List of Characters in
## "Grace"

*Mr. Tom Kernan:* The central character of the story, Kernan is an alcoholic whom his friends have decided to rehabilitate. Tom has had an embarrassing fall in a local bar during which he may have bitten off a small part of his tongue. A converted Protestant, Kernan finally agrees to join his friends at a spiritual retreat.

*Mr. Power:* This friend finds Kernan by chance in the bar where he has fallen. Power intercedes for Kernan with the policeman and takes Kernan home in a cab. It is Power's idea that he and other friends of Kernan should help Tom mend his ways.

*Mr. Martin Cunningham:* An older friend to both Power and Kernan, Cunningham has received the sympathy of all who know him because of the difficulties caused by his alcoholic wife. He is the perfect person to direct Kernan's rehabilitation. Cunningham is respected for his sensibility as well as his intelligence. He directs the conversation at Kernan's house to keep Tom's attention focused on the retreat that his friends have proposed.

*Mr. M'Coy:* Another friend of Kernan's, M'Coy, formerly a tenor of some reputation, has had several occupations. Presently he is the secretary to the City Coroner and as such is interested in Kernan's physical condition after his mishap. M'Coy helps Cunningham in the general plot to help Tom by agreeing with him at regular intervals during their conversations.

*Mrs. Kernan:* Once enthusiastic at the sight of a newly married bride, Mrs. Kernan has learned from experience of the disappointments that marriage brings. She is a capable woman who has managed to bring up her children despite the problems caused by her husband's drinking. Mrs. Kernan agrees to let the men persuade her husband to attend the retreat.

*Harford:* A moneylender in town, Harford has a bad reputation not only for his lending policies but for his frequent visits to the bars. He was with Kernan at the time of his accident but left Kernan on his own.

*Mr. Fogarty:* The local grocer shows a certain amount of grace in his behavior, especially when the neighborhood women shop at his store. Fogarty comes by to visit Kernan when the other men are already discussing the retreat. They all share the bottle of whiskey that Fogarty brings.

*Father Purdon:* The Jesuit holds a spiritual retreat at a local church. Father Purdon tells the men in attendance that since they are businessmen his sermon is directed to them so that they can bring their spiritual accounts back into order. ✸

# Critical Views on
## "Grace"

ROBERT GATES ON "GRACE" AND THE BOOK OF JOB

[Professor Gates is the author of *An Anthology of 18th and 19th Century American Plays*. In this excerpt, Gates concentrates on the sermon delivered by Father Purdon to outline the similarities he finds between "Grace" and the Book of Job. Gates maintains that both God and Purdon appeal to their listeners for "manliness" and that both use a businesslike approach in their address.]

The third and final sections of the Book of Job and "Grace" are also quite similar. Job is concluded with God's appearance in a tempest and His summary of Divine power. The contemporary Kernan and his buddies settle for a sermon delivered by Father Purdon at the Jesuit Church in Gardiner Street.

A number of similarities are easily noticed. God's appearance as a massive tempest in Job (38:1) is comically reflected in Father Purdon, a heavyset man with a "massive red face." When God and Father Purdon speak, the invalids and their friends are shifted to the background of our attention. The once defiant and feisty Job becomes meek and submissive saying, "I put my finger to my lips./I have spoken once and now will not answer again" (Job 40:4-5). And the once defiant Kernan, who enjoyed giving side-thrusts at Catholicism, now becomes submissive, presenting "an attentive face to the preacher." Both invalids are also at "home" in their surroundings. Job is addressed sitting among the ashes he has been confined to during the story, and as Kernan recognizes familiar faces in the congregation he begins to "feel more at home." Finally, both invalids are last seen in a materially restored condition; Job is again blessed with a sizable estate of "fourteen thousand head of cattle and six thousand camels, a thousand yoke of oxen and as many she asses" (Job 42:12-14), while on a less grand level, Kernan's silk hat has been "rehabilitated" by his practical wife.

Far more important, however, is the similarity between the sermon delivered by God and that of Purdon, and the failure of both sermons to resolve the important issues confronted in these stories.

Both God and Purdon make an appeal for "manliness" among those they address. God begins his lecture by first demanding of Job, "Brace yourself and stand up like a man." In a similar vein, Purdon asks his congregation "to be straight and manly with God."

Both God and Purdon then deliver a "businesslike" sermon. God literally presents Job with an accountant's list of all of His accomplishments and abilities. "Where were you," He asks Job, "when I laid the earth's foundations. . . . Who watched over the birth of the sea, when it burst in flood from the womb?" (Job 38:4-8). God is essentially asking Job to tally his achievements against those of the Almighty, and Job is found sadly lacking.

A similar businesslike posture is adopted by Father Purdon, an official representative of God in the twentieth century:

> He came to speak to business men and he would speak to them in a businesslike way. If he might use the metaphor, he said, he was their spiritual accountant; and he wished each and every one of his hearers to open his books, the books of his spiritual life, and see if they tallied accurately with conscience.

—Robert A. Gates, "Tom Kernan and Job." *James Joyce Quarterly* 19 (Spring 1982): pp. 275–288.

## CHERYL HERR ON THE SERMON'S MEANING IN THE STORY

[Professor Herr, the author of *For the Land They Loved*, uses the sermon in "Grace" as a point of departure to study Joyce's handling of the financial enterprises of the church. In this extract, Herr proposes that the sermon was the church's vehicle to establish compatibility between the business world and its religious teachings.]

In that both the style and the content of popularized sermons seem to have irritated Joyce, both informal delivery and uninformed preacher receive attention in "Grace." Skepticism over the doctrine aside, he appears to have objected to any job poorly done and especially to sermons that reflected only the lowest state of the art. This ineffectuality is linked explicitly in the story with sermons that do not differentiate theological doctrine from sound financial methods, for "Grace" shows us the harmony of the business world with the religious teachings available for popular consumption.

From the outset of the story we are led to see that religious conversion is not the answer to the Kernan's problems. Proud of being a tea taster and commercial traveler, the once-successful protagonist has been destroyed not so much by drink as by changes in the economic environment: "Modern business methods had spared him only so far as to allow him a little office in Crowe Street on the window blind of which was written the name of his firm with the address—London, E.C." Like an out-of-date Jehovah, Mr. Kernan passes judgment, spitting teas into the grate. Directly following the description of Kernan's background and job, the narrative introduces the aptly named Mr. Power, the "much younger man" who rescued Tom when he drunkenly fell down the stairs and who is employed, like Martin Cunningham, in Dublin Castle. That the "arc of his social rise intersected the arc of his friend's decline" is significant because those two trajectories describe both the access to power provided by political employment and the inevitable failure of those who have not made the economic choices necessary for survival in the modern business world, even in the seemingly casual way in which that world established itself in early twentieth-century Dublin. Not religion but economics has defined Mr. Kernan's obsolescence and his family's rude poverty.

The relationship of the church to social change is playfully suggested at the story's opening by several uses of the word "curate." This slang term for bartender appears to have amused Joyce (compare the playbill in *Finnegans Wake* in which Saunderson is described as a "spoilcurate" and implies the church's role in a modernizing world, for the curates first set up Tom Kernan for his fall by serving him liquor and then cover up the evidence of the fall ("a curate set about removing the traces of blood from the floor"). Like Father Purdon, whose discourse on grace ignores the doctrine of original sin, these secular curates efface the signs of Kernan's decline. What they have to offer addresses the causes and cures of Kernan's woes as poorly as Father Purdon does.

The economic relationships that define the state of affairs in the story surface in many details. For instance, we are led to believe that

Mrs. Kernan is kept from thinking the emblematic Mr. Power responsible for her husband's dismal state by "remembering Mr. Power's good offices during domestic quarrels as well as many small, but opportune loans." Mr. Fogarty, the grocer whom Kernan owes money, has already "failed in business in a licensed house in the city because his financial condition had constrained him to tie himself to second-class distillers and brewers." Mr. M'Coy is mildly ostracized because he mooches off his friends, and Mr. Harford the financier is quietly censured because he charges usurious rates to lend money to the workers and failing businesspeople of Dublin. Similarly, the very Jesuits who offer the retreat are presented as not just "an educated order" but also as "the boyos [that] have influence"; as Mr. M'Coy crassly notes, "The Jesuits cater for the upper classes," and Power agrees, "Of course." Such references to the dominating socioeconomic relations are too insistent to be ignored. In this Dublin, money talks, while poverty is both powerless and quietly resentful.

—Cheryl Herr, "The Sermon as Massproduct: 'Grace' and *A Portrait*" in *James Joyce: A Collection of Critical Essays*. Ed. Mary T. Reynolds (Englewood Cliffs, N.J.: Prentice-Hall, Inc., 1993): pp. 81–95.

## HOPE HOWELL HODGKINS ON SALVATION IN "GRACE"

[Hope Howell Hodgkins has written on religious rhetoric and high modernism. Howell Hodgkins believes that Joyce puts forward the powers of religious persuasion more so than the goal of making Kernan an ideal Catholic. Here, though, she explains how "Grace" can be seen as the tale of a drunkard's salvation.]

Of course, "Grace" can be and has been read as a straightforward account of a drunkard's salvation. The first few pages prepare us for an ex-drunkard's testimonial: Kernan drinks too much, is going downhill, and is obviously ready for a miraculous conversion. We first find him in the proper position for a recipient of grace: fallen, "quite helpless," his clothes "smeared with the filth and ooze of the floor on which he had lain, face downwards." He is rescued from the law (the constable) by friends who are instruments of grace, especially by Mr. Power who promises to "make a new man of him."

This Bunyanesque allegory is overshadowed by a literalistic insistence on social forms and appearances—in particular on clothing. Kernan, a tea salesman, affirms the "dignity" of his calling through dress: "He had never been seen in the city without a silk hat of some decency and a pair of gaiters. By grace of these two articles of clothing, he said, a man could always pass muster." It is these emblems of gentlemanly "grace" (a third definition of the title) that are smeared and damaged at the story's beginning, and that will be resurrected by the conclusion, in which we hear that all the gentlemen were

> well-dressed and orderly. The light of the lamps of the church fell upon an assembly of black clothes and white collars, relieved here and there by tweeds. . . . The gentlemen sat in the benches, having hitched their trousers slightly above their knees and laid their hats in security.

While Mr. Kernan's concern for his hat, and the general stress on "gentlemanliness," might be read (with a little strain) as illustrative of his inner state, the weight of the narrative goes against such a reading. These are not Christian's spotless garments; like the English drunkard's "fruits of teetotalism," they are the material rewards of earthly effort. And they signify, if anything, the appearances that will blind the protagonist to all but the materialistic temporizing of the priest's closing exhortation to settle his accounts with God.

> —Hope Howell Hodgkins, " 'Just a little . . . spiritual matter': Joyce's 'Grace' and the Modern Protestant Gentleman." *Studies in Short Fiction 32* (Summer 1995): pp. 423–434.

## RICHARD KAIN ON "GRACE" AND *ULYSSES*

[Richard M. Kain, Professor Emeritus from the University of Louisville, has published extensively on both Yeats and Joyce. In this extract, Kain reviews the association between characters found in "Grace" and *Ulysses*. In particular, Kain considers Kernan, Martin Cunningham, and M'Coy in

[*"Grace" and suggests connections between their roles in the short story and specific character manifestations in *Ulysses*.]

'Grace' shares with 'Ivy Day in the Committee Room' the feeling of being a study for *Ulysses*, which, we recall, was first conceived as a story for *Dubliners*. Both these stories have a strong sense of milieu, that reek of the streets and shabby buildings which permeates *Ulysses*, and both have the same sense of character. Casual links between 'Ivy Day' and 'Grace' can be seen in that two members of the congregation at the retreat, Mr. Fanning and Michael Grimes, are referred to in the political discussion of the earlier story. More prominent is the role of Crofton in both stories, as a respectful opponent of Parnell in 'Ivy Day' and in a similar role of dignified opposition as the 'damned decent Orangeman' here.

These two stories contribute more characters to *Ulysses* than any others do, though in this respect 'Grace' is of greater importance. First, Kernan. Throughout the day Bloom has in mind getting tea from him, but characteristically forgets to ask. On the way to the funeral Cunningham ridicules his pompous manner of speech— 'trenchant rendering' and 'retrospective arrangement' are key phrases—and when Mr. Power asks about Fogarty Simon Dedalus replies, 'Better ask Tom Kernan', the innuendo being that the pot-washing in 'Grace' was of brief effect. In Glasnevin cemetery he is in character as a skeptical Catholic, expressing a preference for the liturgy of the Church of Ireland. He walks the streets of Dublin later in the day ('Wandering Rocks'), happy over the order he has booked, and preens himself before a shop mirror. At the Ormond Hotel ('Sirens') he finds Ben Dollard's singing of 'The Croppy Boy' sufficiently 'trenchant'. Finally Molly Bloom recalls with disgust the episode at the pub: 'that drunken little barrelly man that bit his tongue off falling down the mens WC drunk in some place or other . . .'

Martin Cunningham, who engineers the scheme for getting Kernan to the retreat, plays a subsidiary role of considerable importance in *Ulysses*. He is there characterized by Father John Conmee as a 'Good practical catholic: useful at mission time', and lives up to this description in his efforts to raise a fund for Paddy Dignam's widow. He is also sensitive to the discussion of suicide in the funeral carriage, realizing that Bloom's father had poisoned himself. Bloom had concocted a scheme to get a pass through Cunningham, but that never eventuated. There is no need to follow him through *Ulysses*, nor his companion

Jack Power. Both, incidentally, have marital difficulties, Cunningham's wife being an alcoholic, and Power maintaining a barmaid. Together with Crofton, they effect Bloom's escape from the ireful Citizen at Barney Kiernan's. The fact that these characters play so extensive a part in *Ulysses* suggests the possibility that the unwritten story for *Dubliners* may have become transposed into the funeral chapter and the 'Wandering Rocks' episode of the novel.

Long John Fanning also appears briefly, as does M'Coy, again at the old dodge described in 'Grace', namely 'a crusade in search of valises and portmanteaus to enable Mrs. M'Coy to fulfil imaginary engagements in the country.' Bloom remembers the valise trick several times during the day of *Ulysses*, having lost one he specially liked, but he also thinks of working M'Coy for a pass. On meeting Bloom in the morning, M'Coy had asked him to put down his name as attending the funeral. Though Bloom is disconcerted at meeting him, he does do this favour, with the result that the *Evening Telegraph* erroneously reports him as attending the service. Thus four of the five penitents, all but Fogarty, are associated with the funeral of Paddy Dignam.

—Richard M. Kain, "Grace" in *Twentieth Century Interpretations of "Dubliners."* Ed. Peter K. Garrett (Englewood Cliffs, N.J.: Prentice-Hall, Inc., 1968): pp. 134–152.

THOMAS RICE ON THE PUBLICATION OF *DUBLINERS*

[Thomas J. Rice's most recent book is entitled *Joyce, Chaos, and Complexity* (1997). Here Professor Rice discusses the delay in the publication of *Dubliners* and the critical interpretations of paralysis in its short stories. Rice begins his essay with this excerpt where he outlines the arrangement of the stories and quotes Joyce's comments on the structure in letters to his brother, Stanislaus, and the publisher Grant Richards.]

In late September 1905 James Joyce wrote from Trieste to his brother Stanislaus in Dublin, requesting (as ever) some personal favors and describing for the first time his plan for arranging the short stories that would eventually become Dubliners in a coherent sequence:

The order of the stories is as follows. *The Sisters, An Encounter* and another story ["Araby"] which are stories of my childhood. *The Boarding House, After the Race* and *Eveline,* which are stories of adolescence: *The Clay, Counterparts,* and *A Painful Case* which are stories of mature life: *Ivy Day in the Committee Room, A Mother* and the last story of the book ["Grace'] which are stories of public life in Dublin. (Letters 2:111)

During October and November Joyce composed "Araby" and "Grace," the two remaining stories of this original 12-story sequence, and reversed the order of his stories of "adolescence." At the end of November 1905, he mailed this early version of *Dubliners* to the English publisher Grant Richards, little suspecting that he would endure nearly a year of frustrating and ultimately futile negotiation for their publication. On 26 October 1906 Richards, who feared that both he and his printer could be prosecuted for publishing an "indecent" book, finally returned Joyce's manuscript (which had grown to 14 stories in the interim with the addition of "Two Gallants" and "A Little Cloud").

What chiefly interests me in this "Curious History" of the publication delays for *Dubliners,* as Joyce called it (*Letters* 2:324), is not the often exaggerated story it tells of Joyce's defense of his artistic integrity, nor the lesson it offers on the power of censorship, but rather the way Joyce's descriptions of his artistic intentions in his letters to Richards in 1905–06 have entered and come to dominate the critical discussion of Joyce's short fiction. Midway in his correspondence with Richards, for example, on 5 May 1906, Joyce identified a central theme in his work, defined his literary style, defended his refusal to compromise either his text or his artistic conscience, and once again described his conception of the four-part arrangement of the stories:

> My intention was to write a chapter of the moral history of my country and I chose Dublin for the scene because that city seemed to me the centre of paralysis. I have tried to present it to the indifferent public under four of its aspects: childhood, adolescence, maturity and public life. The stories are arranged in this order. I have written it for the most part in a style of scrupulous meanness and with the conviction that he is a very bold man who dares to alter in the presentment, still more to deform, whatever he has seen and heard. I cannot do any more than this. I cannot alter what I have written. (*Letters* 2:134)

> —Thomas Jackson Rice, "Paradigm Lost: 'Grace' and the Arrangement of *Dubliners.*" *Studies in Short Fiction* 32 (Summer 1995): pp. 405–421. ☙

# Plot Summary of
## "The Dead"

Regarded as Joyce's best short fiction, "The Dead" was finished in the spring of 1907. Because of its length and complexity, the story can be considered a novella. The narrative voice of the story allows the reader to follow the action closely as well as to understand the characters' thoughts and sentiments.

"Lily, the caretaker's daughter, was literally run off her feet." The exhaustion Lily feels is matched only by the overall exuberance and energy abounding in the Morkan sisters' home as everyone anticipates their annual New Year's dinner dance. Kate and Julia, the elderly Morkan sisters, headed the festivities that for years had never failed to please. Their niece, Mary Jane, whose music pupils would be in attendance, helped with the preparations. Though the women lived modestly, they lived well. Lily, the housemaid, was a conscientious worker who seldom made a mistake to upset her mistresses. "They were fussy, that was all. But the only thing they would not stand was back answers."

Lily's exhaustion was due in part to attending to the gentlemen as they arrived. But more so it was a result of calling up to her mistresses who tended the women upstairs. It was already past 10 o'clock on a snowy evening and the Morkan women were waiting for the arrival of Gabriel Conroy and his wife, Gretta. They were worried as well that Freddy Malins would show up intoxicated and they knew that only Gabriel could control him in such a state. When, at last, Gabriel and Gretta arrived, Kate and Julia came downstairs to greet their favorite nephew and his wife. Soon the three women disappeared to the ladies' dressing room on the next floor, while Gabriel started cleaning the snow from his boots. As he did, he and Lily spoke amiably but when Gabriel implied that she was old enough to have a young man, the tone of their conversation changed. Gabriel, a stout and tallish young man, blushed as he thought of the mistake he had just made. He paid closer attention to his shoes and gave Lily a coin for Christmas as he left the room.

A waltz could be heard from the drawing room since the dance was already in full swing. When Julia announced that Freddy was there, Kate summoned Gabriel to check on his condition. Kate told Mrs. Conroy that she was relieved that Gabriel was there. Then Kate directed Julia to get some refreshments for their guests and to bring Mr. Browne and Miss Furlong in particular into the drawing room. Mr. Browne, a "tall wizenfaced man" was then left on his own with the young women near him. As he filled his glass with whiskey, Browne assured both the women and the young men in attendance that he was following doctor's orders. In the meantime, Gabriel directed Freddy, a man of about forty, past the aunts. Freddy greeted them heartily but when he noticed Mr. Browne, Freddy crossed the room and began to tell him the same story he had just finished telling Gabriel.

Mary Jane began to play her "academy piece" for all in attendance. Gabriel found it difficult to listen. Instead he stared at a picture of the balcony scene in *Romeo and Juliet* that hung in the room. Not far away was a picture of Gabriel's deceased mother, Ellen, the eldest Morkan sister. When Mary Jane finished playing, a dance was arranged and Gabriel was partnered with Miss Ivors, a talkative young woman with a freckled face. Miss Ivors was known to speak frankly and when they waited to join the dance she confronted Gabriel with the fact that she knew he wrote for a paper she did not admire. As Gabriel's face flushed, she confessed she was only teasing and then asked Gabriel if he would like to join an excursion that summer. When Gabriel questioned her why she and her friends did not want to tour through Ireland, the conversation became a bit agitated. At the end of the dance, Gabriel retreated to a corner of the room.

As dinnertime approached, Gabriel had a difficult time paying any attention to what was said to him. Instead, he concentrated on the speech he would make. Gabriel wondered though if Miss Ivors had been sincere when she praised his writing. He decided to make an allusion to their conversation in his speech thinking that his aunts would not notice since "his aunts were only two ignorant old women." As the room filled, Julia sang "Arrayed for the Bridal" in a strong and clear voice. Gabriel approached the end of the table where the goose lay since his aunts wanted him to manage the carving. It took some doing but finally everyone was served. Gabriel did not converse with the others, among them Mr. Bartell D'Arcy, a tenor currently performing at the Theatre Royal. Mary Jane directed those at the table in a discussion about the opera. Many commented on whom they considered to be the best tenor. Kate finally announced that for her Parkinson was the best. The younger guests at the table did not recognize the name but Mr. Browne agreed with her choice.

After the fruit and chocolates and sweets were served, it was time for Gabriel's speech. His bold beginning provoked assent around the table:

—I feel more strongly with every recurring year that our country has no tradition which does it so much honour and which it should guard so jealously as that of its hospitality.

But Gabriel lamented the new generation of Irish who, in his view, were growing up without a belief in such a traditional and national value. He shifted the talk to toast the Morkan women whom Gabriel called "the three Graces of the Dublin musical world." All applauded with great enthusiasm while "Aunt Kate was making frank use of her handkerchief and even aunt Julia seemed moved."

The scene changed to one of farewells at the front door. Gabriel was dressing for the cold night outside while at the same time Mrs. Malins was waiting for her son Freddy to join her as Mr. Browne tried to give directions to the cabbie. When Gabriel looked for his wife, he noticed her standing quietly on the second floor landing. Gretta was listening to a singing Bartell D'Arcy, who had not wanted to perform for the entire gathering because of a bad throat. The Conroys said their goodbyes at the door and started walking for a cab. "She was walking on before him so lightly and so erect that he longed to run after her noiselessly, catch her by the shoulders and say something foolish and affectionate into her ear. She seemed to him so frail that he longed to defend her against something and then to be alone with her. Moments of their secret life together burst like stars upon his memory."

They shared a cab with Miss O'Callaghan and Mr. D'Arcy. At their hotel, Gabriel insisted on paying the driver. His thoughts of Gretta grew more passionate and when the porter lead them to their hotel room, Gabriel told him to take away the candle because the light from the street would be enough for them. Gretta moved slowly and seemed tired, which annoyed Gabriel. "He was trembling now with annoyance. Why did she seem so abstracted? He did not know how he could begin. Was she annoyed too about something? If she would only turn to him or come to him of her own accord! To take her as she was would be brutal. No, he must see some ardour in her eyes first. He longed to be master of her strange mood."

Surprisingly, Gretta approached him and kissed him lightly. Gabriel was greatly encouraged by her action but finally asked his wife why she was so pensive. Gretta told him the song "The Lass of Aughrim" was occupying her mind. It reminded her of Michael Furey, a young boy she knew when she was a girl. Michael was a delicate boy with whom Gretta would go walking. She confessed to Gabriel that Michael had died at the age of seventeen because of her. When Gabriel asked if Gretta was in love with him, she replied that she "was great with him at that time." She sobbed, face down on the bed, as she recounted the story of Michael's death. Gabriel held her hand and then realized she had fallen fast asleep.

As Gabriel reflected on her story, he peered out of the hotel window. It was snowing again. "It was falling, too, upon every part of the lonely churchyard on the hill where Michael Furey lay buried. It lay thickly drifted on the crooked crosses and headstones, on the spears of the little gate, on the barren thorns. His soul swooned slowly as he heard the snow falling faintly through the universe and faintly falling, like the descent of their last end, upon all the living and the dead." ❀

# List of Characters in
## "The Dead"

*Gabriel Conroy:* The principal character of the story, Gabriel is the center of attention for several reasons. He is his aunts' favorite nephew, he is the only one who can control Freddy Malins's unpredictable behavior, and he has planned to deliver a speech to all in attendance at the New Year's dinner dance held annually by his aunts, Kate and Julia Morkan. As the story closes, Gabriel gazes at the snow falling outside his room and contemplates his connections to both the living and the dead.

*Gretta Conroy:* The wife of Gabriel, Gretta has caused them to arrive late because she takes so long to dress. She reveals to her husband at the end of the evening that a song has made her remember a young boy of whom she was quite fond. Gretta shares her sadness with Gabriel as she recounts the unhappy tale of the young man's untimely death.

*Kate Morkan:* Kate was feeble from age and so gave music lessons from home. Like her sister, Julia, she doted on their nephew, Gabriel, who was the son of their older sister, Ellen. She counted on Gabriel to keep Freddy Malins in line during the party.

*Julia Morkan:* Though advanced in years, Julia still sang the leading soprano part with a local music group. On her sister's direction, Julia tended to their guests and made sure they had all the refreshments they needed during the dance.

*Mary Jane:* The only niece of the Morkan sisters, she went to live with them when quite young. Mary Jane gives music lessons to young Dubliners, several of whom are in attendance at the New Year's party. For the group's entertainment, Mary Jane plays an intricate piano piece.

*Lily:* This is the Morkan sisters' housemaid. She is conscientious to please them and their niece, Mary Jane. Lily, though normally polite, has a sharp remark for Gabriel when he suggests she is old enough to have a suitor.

*Miss Ivors:* She is a frank-speaking and talkative young woman with a freckled face and brown eyes. Miss Ivors tell Gabriel that she admired his writing. But they have a disagreement when they discuss her plans to go on an excursion outside of Ireland.

*Mr. Browne:* A bit of a ladies' man, this wizen-faced man adds whiskey to the lemonade and enjoys a tall tale related to him by Freddy Malins.

*Freddy Malins:* The young man regularly caused the Morkan sisters concern because of his excessive drinking. Kate asked her nephew, Gabriel, to keep Freddy in line during the evening's festivities.

*Mr. Bartell D'Arcy:* A famous tenor, at the time of the Morkans' dinner, D'Arcy was performing at the Theatre Royal.

*Michael Furey:* A young delicate boy who died at the age of seventeen, Michael was in love with Gretta before she left for convent-school in Dublin. He used to sing the song, "The Lass of Aughrim." Though he was sick and confined to his bed, on the night before Gretta left for Dublin, he had stood wet and shivering outside her window. ❀

# Critical Views on
## "The Dead"

### THOMAS DILWORTH ON GABRIEL CONROY'S NAME

[Professor Dilworth from the University of Windsor separates "The Dead" into two parts: the party at which Gabriel Conroy delivers his speech and the conclusion when Gabriel senses his connections with the living and the dead. In this excerpt, Dilworth traces the etymology of Gabriel's surname in order to examine its political implications in the story.]

The surname "Conroy" has a false and a true etymology. The Gaelic original is MacConroi, which means "hound of the plain, or of the battlefield." But since the seventeenth century it has often mistakenly been translated into English as "King" because in Gaelic the surname is homonymous with the Irish "*Mac an Righ*," which means "Son of the King." The true etymology of the name was known and in print by the mid-nineteenth century. But the popular misconception was widespread until well into the twentieth century. According to Patrick Woulfe in the first quarter of this century, the name Conroy is "usually mistranslated 'King.'" In the *Irish Registry of Births, Deaths and Marriages* for 1901, Conroy and King are listed as synonyms: births in families surnamed Conroy are also registered under the name King.

In "The Dead," the false etymology of Gabriel's surname seems echoed in various words and phrases: "the Theatre Royal," "The Royal University" at which Gabriel took his degree, the sovereign Gabriel receives from Freddy Malins. All such references are actually, albeit obliquely, to English royalty, of course, and this in itself has implications for an Irishman whose patronymic supposedly means "Son of the King." The name may imply loyalty to the English king, but since the name is Irish, perhaps the most powerful implications are of usurpation and abdication. In *Ulysses*, Mr. Deasy says, "We are all Irish, all kings' sons," and Stephen answers, "Alas." Stephen realizes what I think we are meant to realize when Gabriel says during his dinner speech that if hospitality is a failing with the Irish, "it is, to my mind, a princely failing." Conroy's being a prince or a king in any sense, even a false sense, suggests that he has a symbolic relationship to Ireland and that this relationship is essentially political.

The symbolism of Gabriel's surname correlates, furthermore, with the symbolic character of the feast over which he presides. The Misses Morkan's party takes place after New Year's Eve, yet within "the Christmas." The only festival after New Year's and within the Twelve Days of Christmas is the evening of January fifth, Twelfth Night. The date of the Morkans' party cannot be precisely determined, but whatever its exact date, the party seems symbolically to correspond to the Twelfth Night celebration. If the party actually does take place on that night, then Gabriel's epiphany of failure and mortality occurs in the early "morning" hours of January sixth, the feast of Epiphany. In any case, the symbolism of Gabriel's surname recalls that the original epiphany was made to Magi regarded in Christian folklore as kings. But it is in the context of the traditional celebration of Twelfth Night that the false, popular etymology behind Conroy's association with kingship has its richest implications.

—Thomas Dilworth, "Sex and Politics in 'The Dead.'" *James Joyce Quarterly 23* (Winter 1986): pp. 157–171.

## C. C. LOOMIS JR. ON GABRIEL'S EPIPHANY

[In this extract, C. C. Loomis scrutinizes the character of Gabriel in Joyce's text that he divides into five sections: the musicale, the dinner, the farewells, the scene between Gabriel and Gretta, and the vision. Loomis believes that Joyce's challenge is to induce the reader to sympathize with Gabriel so that objective truth might lead to an objective sympathy.]

Gabriel's epiphany manifests Joyce's fundamental belief that true, objective perception will lead to true, objective sympathy; such perception and such sympathy, however, ultimately defy intellectual analysis. Joyce carefully avoids abstract definition of Gabriel's vision by embodying it within the story's central symbol: the snow, which becomes paradoxicaly warm in the moment of vision, through which Gabriel at long last feels the deeply unifying bond of common mortality.

Gabriel's experience is intellectual only at that level on which intellect and emotional intuition blend, and the full power of the story can be apprehended by the reader only if he sympathetically shares the experience with Gabriel. As understanding of himself, then of his world, then of humanity floods Gabriel, so understanding of Gabriel, his world, and humanity in terms of the story floods the reader. The understanding in both cases is largely emotional and intuitive; intellectual analysis of the snow symbol, however successful, leaves a large surplus of emotion unexplained.

Therefore, Joyce had to generate increasing reader-sympathy as he approached the vision, but this sympathy could not be generated by complete reader-identification with Gabriel. If the reader identifies himself unreservedly with Gabriel in the first ninety percent of the story, he will lose that critical insight into him which is necessary for full apprehension of his vision. It is, after all, Gabriel's vision, and there is no little irony in this fact. The vision is in sharp contrast with his previous view of the world: in fact, it literally opens a new world to him. If the reader identifies himself uncritically with Gabriel at any point in the story, he is liable to miss those very shortcomings which make the vision meaningful. Yet, in the actual moments of vision, the reader must share Gabriel's view; in a real sense, he must identify himself with Gabriel: "feel with" him.

—C. C. Loomis Jr., "Structure and Sympathy in Joyce's 'The Dead'" in *PMLA* 75 (March 1960): pp. 149–151.

## L. J. Morrissey on "The Dead" and "Araby"

[L. J. Morrissey taught courses on 18th and 20th century fiction and literary theory before his death in 1987. In this study, he examines Gabriel, his relationship with Gretta, and images of snow. Here, Morrissey begins his analysis by comparing Gabriel to the young boy in "Araby," concluding that both males are defeated by "a simple Irish female."]

Gabriel is not an innocent like the boy. Instead, from the beginning of the story, he feels alienated from his culture and insecure as a result of his alienation. That is, he feels superior because "the indelicate clacking of the men's heels and the shuffling of their soles reminded him that their grade of culture differed from his." Yet he feels inadequate before them. "He would only make himself ridiculous.... He would fail with them...." His inner image of his wife is comprised of a similar vacillation. He is delighted by her exterior image at the opening of the party; his "admiring and happy eyes had been wandering from her dress to her face and her hair." Yet his attained ideal is corrupted by a nagging doubt, by a fear that, as his Mother said, she is only "country cute." When she gently mocks Gabriel's continental affectation about goloshes with her Irish phrasing—"Tonight even he wanted me to put them on," "Gutta-percha things"—he reminds her of her "grade of culture": "Gabriel knitted his brows and said, as if he were slightly angered: It's nothing very wonderful but Gretta thinks it very funny because she says the word reminds her of Christy Minstrels." Put in her place, Gretta falls silent. His ideal woman will no longer break into vulgar "peal[s] of laughter."

Nearly the same pattern is repeated at the end of the party. First Gabriel sees Gretta as a romantic image from a painting. Distanced and silenced by Bartell D'Arcy's singing of "The Lass of Aughrim," she has been so self-effaced, so "unaware of the talk about her," that Aunt Julia nearly misses her when the good-nights are said: "O, good-night, Gretta, I didn't see you." Because she is so silent, Gabriel can continue his romantic revery despite the "murky air" of Dublin. He can nearly ignore that with "her shoes in a brown parcel tucked under one arm and her hands holding her skirt up from the slush [s]he had no longer any grace of attitude." Like the boy in "Araby" he can take his romantic image into the squalid Dublin night and yet keep the romance alive. By editing the "[m]oments of their secret life together [which] burst like stars upon his memory," he can "forget the years of their dull existence together and remember only their moments of ecstasy." Again, like "Araby," this inner romantic image of the male is brought down by the inner yearning of a simple Irish female.

—L. J. Morrissey, "Inner and Outer Perceptions in Joyce's 'The Dead.'" *Studies in Short Fiction* 25 (Winter 1988): pp. 21–29.

SANDRA MANOOGIAN PEARCE ON JAMES JOYCE AND
EDNA O'BRIEN

[As well as interviewing Edna O'Brien, Professor Pearce has
published several essays on Joyce. In this comparative study,
Pearce concentrates on the depictions by both writers of
Dublin, its inhabitants, and their activities. The immediate
associations between both stories are outlined in this
excerpt.]

The title story of [Edna] O'Brien's latest collection *Lantern Slides*
places O'Brien even more securely within the Joycean sphere, for now
setting has moved east to Dublin. Gone is the lush Irish countryside;
gone are the proper Connor girls; gone are Cait and Baba. Gone, too,
are the erotic but innocent prelapsarian longings of those protago-
nists reminiscent of Joyce's two West country women, Gretta and
Bertha. In their stead is a dazzling display of Dublin's dinner "nobs."
While richly resonant of Joyce's "The Dead," this party is not con-
sumed with talk of politics, music, or lost loves, but rather with Gucci
ties, tacky poetry, and lost lusts. O'Brien's feminist rewriting of "The
Dead" is delightfully, searingly ironic, but the subtext is even more so,
revealing a satiric pen that blots male and female alike with the same
scathing ink, delivering an indictment that goes far beyond Joyce's.

From the opening paragraph of "Lantern Slides," O'Brien's extension of Joyce's story is glaringly apparent. Gabriel Conroy has become
Mr. Conroy, hotel worker, whatever that means. Mr. Conroy's stories
suggest that he is working in a brothel rather than a hotel. While "The
Dead" evokes lyrical images of faintly falling snow, "Lantern Slides"
opens with imagery more reminiscent of "Circe," in a "big hall" where
in "a big limestone grate, a turf fire blazes." The next few sentences
confirm the story's setting: "The surround was a bit lugubrious, like a
grotto, but this impression was forgotten as the flames spread and
swagged into brazen orange banners. In the sitting room, a further
galaxy of people. . . . Here too was a fire. . .". We are in Hell, the hell of
Dante's *Inferno*, where not only flames assail the body, but also noise
(remember the din of Satan flapping his wings?). Waiters move "like
altar boys among the panting throngs," while people ask "from time to
time how this racket could be quelled, because quelled it would have
to be when the moment came, when the summons for silence came."
But no silence comes, unlike the beautifully haunting silence that ends

"The Dead." Here, openly flirtatious Dr. Fitz will not shut up; outrageously sexist Mr. Gogarty keeps on joking. Even the chandeliers "seem[ed] to be chattering, so dense and busy and clustered were the shining pendants of glass." These "chattering" chandeliers set the tone of the story: we will judge and be judged by gossip, rumor, innuendo, and association.

O'Brien replaces Gretta's impassioned weeping for a lost Michael Furey with Miss Lawless's lustful desires for the newly resurrected appearance of a second Peter Abelard, her lost lover of 25 years earlier (and of course, invoking the original Abelard—twelfth century scholar, monk and lover of Heloise). The Dantesque vision of Gretta/Beatrice enshrouded in the "dusty fanlight" (evoked more fully in John Huston's movie version, in which Gretta stands earlier in the stained-glass stairwell) gives way in O'Brien's story to "patches of sea like diagonals of stained glass," reminding us that the lantern slides are not infused in Dantean light, but clouded with mists of the sea, or shrouded in distant and disjointed memories.

—Sandra Manoogian Pearce, "Edna O'Brien's 'Lantern Slides' and Joyce's 'The Dead': Shadows of a Bygone Era." *Studies in Short Fiction* 32 (Summer 1995): pp. 437–446.

## LIONEL TRILLING ON THE IMPORTANCE OF "THE DEAD"

[In this excerpt, the well-known author and critic Lionel Trilling assesses the importance of "The Dead" in the canon of modern literature. Trilling believes that Gabriel Conroy's sense of a death-in-life has become a commonplace that many readers as well as critics in our day can understand and appreciate. The juxtaposition of Joyce and Gabriel, Trilling maintains, helps to understand the character of Conroy in "The Dead."]

Joyce writes of his own nation and city with passionate particularity. But when we consider the very high place that "The Dead" has been given in the canon of modern literature, and the admiration it has won from readers of the most diverse backgrounds, we must say that

Joyce has written a chapter in the moral history not only of his own country but of the whole modern western world. Gabriel Conroy's plight, his sense that he has been overtaken by death-in-life, is shared by many in our time: it is one of the characteristics of modern society that an ever-growing number of people are not content to live by habit and routine and by the unquestioning acceptance of the circumstances into which they have been born. They believe they have the right to claim for themselves pleasure, or power, or dignity, or fullness of experience; a prerogative which in former times was exercised by relatively few people, usually members of the privileged classes, and which now seems available to many people regardless of class. Yet almost in the degree that modern man feels free to assert the personal claims which are the expression of a heightened sense of individuality, he seems to fall prey to that peculiarly modern disorder so often remarked by novelists, psychologists, and sociologists—an uncertainty about who the person is who makes the claims, a diminished sense of his personal identity.

Identity is the word that Gabriel Conroy uses when he thinks about death: he sees "his own identity . . . fading out into a grey impalpable world." And his imagination of death provides the image of his life. All through the evening his identity had been fading out into the grey impalpable world of his aunts' party. All through his youth and his early middle-age his identity had been fading out into the grey impalpable world of Dublin society.

It is sometimes said that Gabriel Conroy is what James Joyce would have been, or what he supposed he would have been, if he had not fled Dublin at the age of twenty, with no resources but his talent and his youth, risking privation for the sake of achievement and fame. And certainly the juxtaposition of the author and his character helps us understand Gabriel Conroy. Joyce was one of an old and rare species of man: he was a genius, with all the stubborn resistance and courage, all the strong sense of identity, by which, in addition to great gifts, genius is defined. Gabriel Conroy is one of a new, and very numerous, kind of man whose large demand upon life is supported neither by native gift nor moral energy. He has the knowledge of excellence but cannot achieve it for himself; he admires distinction and cannot attain it.

—Lionel Trilling, "Characterization in 'The Dead' " in *James Joyce's "Dubliners": A Critical Handbook.* Eds. James R. Baker and Thomas F. Staley (Belmont, Calif.: Wadsworth Publishing Company, Inc., 1969): pp. 155–159.

# Roland Wagner on Mother and Child in "The Dead"

[Roland C. Wagner, a professor at Hofstra University, has published on Wallace Stevens, as well as Joyce, Svevo, and Forster. Professor Wagner proposes here a relationship between the time of composition of "The Dead" and Joyce's needs at the time in order to suggest the Christian and art-historical ties between the story and the Annunciation theme. In this extract, Wagner discusses Joyce's "identification with mother and child."]

Ellmann writes that Joyce was vitally involved in "all aspects of the bond of mother and child," and he describes how Joyce developed biological metaphors of the creative process in *Stephen Hero*, more fully in *A Portrait of the Artist*, and most elaborately in *Ulysses*.

> This creator is not only male but female; Joyce goes on to borrow an image of Flaubert by calling him a 'god,' but he is also a goddess. Within his womb creatures come to life. Gabriel the seraph comes to the Virgin's chamber and, as Stephen says, "In the virgin womb of the imagination the word is made flesh."

Thus the Gabriel of "The Dead," who we have already seen is the child inside Gretta's body, can also be seen as the mother of that child. The later, major works develop artistically and intellectually what is embodied intuitively in "The Dead." We get a hint of Gabriel's maternal side when we learn that his extreme "solicitude" for their children and for Gretta "was a standing joke with" his aunts. "The next thing he'll buy me [after the galoshes]," Gretta jokes, "will be a diving suit." There is another, different sort of hint at the end as Gabriel draws together the various strands of his life. The softly falling snow, and the water it becomes, deepens into a symbol of purity and primal unity. Pushed outside of Gretta's womb, Gabriel transforms the universe itself into an object of love. Reality, in effect, emerges as the Great Mother or the offspring of the Mother. The cold, cruel world can now be accepted in its divine indifference. His separation is a step toward a new kind of oneness. If Gabriel to a degree transcends his narcissism through his "enlarging identification with the whole mortal life of man," it is partly because the roots of that narcissism are there to serve his newfound but modest capacity for love.

As we begin to appreciate Joyce's youthful conscious and uncon-scious intentions, a much more hidden element in "The Dead" now becomes visible, shedding more light on those intentions and fur-ther serving to clarify Joyce's feelings of identification with mother and child (and father as well). It will also deepen our understanding of Gabriel and his need to idealize and cover up the "western" half of his mind. Standing behind the story throughout—but most spectac-ularly at the moment when Gabriel looks up to the top of the Morkan stairs and sees his wife listening to Mr. D'Arcy singing "The Lass of Aughrim"—is a model for a painting of the Annunciation. In a limited way Joyce was trying to do what the Dutch and Flemish painters were doing in the fifteenth and sixteenth centuries. The method Joyce uses is known in art history as "disguised symbolism," which reflects precisely his purposes in the story and anticipates the method of *Ulysses*. Only the method is far from fully realized here, for it does not really illuminate most of the details of "The Dead." What it does illuminate is the last third of the story, especially at sev-eral highly significant moments.

—Roland C. Wagner, "A Birth Announcement in 'The Dead.'" *Studies in Short Fiction* 32 (Summer 1995): pp. 447–462.

## Craig Werner on Gabriel Conroy

[Craig H. Werner focuses on Gabriel Conroy in this extract. Although Gabriel moves with relative ease in the masculine world, he notes a series of self-imposed failures with females that lead to an emotional epiphany in the final scene of the story. According to Professor Werner, Joyce successfully estab-lishes sympathy and distance between Gabriel and the reader.]

Contrasting with his self-defined "defeats" at the hands of Lily ("he felt he had made a mistake") and Molly Ivors ("She had tried to make him ridiculous before people"), Gabriel experiences several moments of triumph. Both his speech and his retelling of the story of Johnny the horse heighten his sense of satisfaction. Watching Gretta listen to Bartell D'Arcy's singing, Gabriel leaves the party with a feeling of aesthetic exhilaration despite the earlier disruptions. As Gabriel and Gretta return to the hotel where they will spend the night away from their children, Gabriel feels intense sexual desire and envisions a romantic climax to the evening. Completing the pattern of egoistic triumph and equally egoistic defeat, Gabriel's fantasy collapses in the face of Gretta's actual experience. D'Arcy's song—"The Lass of Aughrim"—turns Gretta's thoughts toward Michael Furey, who had courted her during her youth in the west of Ireland. Acutely disappointed and jealous of the shadowy Michael, Gabriel can do little save listen and wait for his wife to fall asleep. In a story populated by an abundance of ghosts—of singers, King William, Daniel O'Connell, the two Patrick Morkans, Gabriel's mother Ellen—the dead youth is more real to the Conroys than any living person.

As Gretta sleeps beside him, Gabriel experiences an epiphany of his own connection with the living dead. One of the most famous concluding passages in modern literature, Gabriel's epiphany reflects his weariness at the end of a long and emotionally exhausting day. Like the conclusions of "Araby" and "A Painful Case," Gabriel's epiphany reflects his sudden awareness of his own egoism. Unlike Duffy or the disillusioned youth, however, Gabriel places this recognition in the context of a widening circle of connections:

> The time had come for him to set out on his journey westward. Yes, the newspapers were right: snow was general all over Ireland. It was falling on every part of the dark central plain, on the treeless hills, falling softly upon the Bog of Allen and, farther westward, softly falling into the dark mutinous Shannon waves. It was falling, too, upon every part of the lonely churchyard on the hill where Michael Furey lay buried. It lay thickly drifted on the crooked crosses and headstones, on the spears of the little gate, on the barren thorns. His soul swooned slowly as he heard the snow falling faintly through the universe and faintly falling, like the descent of their last end, upon all the living and the dead.

One in a sequence of epiphanies occurring toward the end of "The Dead," this passage is written in the mature style Joyce had perfected during the writing of *Dubliners*. The story's effectiveness hinges on Joyce's ability to establish both close sympathy and ironic distance between the reader and Gabriel. He accomplishes this delicate balance through a gradually accelerating dramatic rhythm combined with subtle modulations in the style of individual sentences.

—Craig Hansen Werner, "Gabriel's Process" in *"Dubliners": A Pluralistic World*. (Boston: Twayne Publishers, 1988): pp. 59–60.

# Critical Views on
## James Joyce and *Dubliners*

BERNARD BENSTOCK ON THE GNOMONICS OF *DUBLINERS*

[Bernard Benstock, a well-known Joyce scholar, is the author of *James Joyce: The Augmented Ninth*. Professor Benstock discusses here, among other gnomonics, the physical and spiritual presence of priests in the three *Dubliners* childhood stories. In the extract, Benstock summarizes the presences and the absences of the gnomons throughout the collection. He suggests a circular construct on the part of Joyce by beginning with "The Sisters" and closing with "The Dead."]

The gnomons that abound in *Dubliners*—or would abound if they were not so blatantly missing—reflect the narrative strategies of the stories: absence of climatic instances, deleted resolutions of plot, inconclusive closures, inexact overlays of perception on the part of the characters, insufficient information about them: so that Maria has no family name and Farrington no given name, and the boy in the first three stories no names at all (although we know that the boy in "An Encounter" cannot be named Smith because that is the alias he designates for himself), and so trivial a character as the railway company representative in "A Painful Case" is fully equipped with a handle like "Mr. H. B. Patterson Finlay." Nominations are gnomonic ("Sounds are impostures," Stephen Dedalus contends; "FOR time. Like names READ time, like names. . . . What's in a name?" [*Ulysses* 16. 362–364]), and Farrington is often referred to in the text as "the man," yet in losing his wrestling match with Weathers he is unmanned, becoming a Noman. Many another male in Dubliners is deprived of his full masculinity: Bob Doran at the hands of the Mooney women; Mr. Kearney in the hands of a determined wife with ivory manners; Gabriel Conroy, a self-styled Romantic Man, deflated by the intrusion into his life of the ghostly Michael Furey, a stripling long-dead who had long outdistanced him as a lover. And Little Chandler, already in trouble with his wife for having forgotten to bring home "the parcel of coffee from Bewley's," is further demeaned when she returns to find their baby wailing. Turning her back on her husband ("Giving no heed to him"), she concentrates her attention exclusively on the child, calling the infant "My little man! My little mannie!"

The word gnomon comes from the Greek, meaning "interpreter, discerner, pointer on a sundial, a carpenter's square." The most pointed indicators as such in *Dubliners* are the story titles, the first indications in each instance. The book title designates an entire population and by internal reference a place of residence, yet the parts that stand for the whole are the handful of Dubliners actually delineated in the fifteen stories. Of the story titles, some pinpoint characters ("The Sisters," "Eveline," "Two Gallants," "A Mother"); others a place ("Araby," "The Boarding House," "Ivy Day in the Committee Room")' one a time-frame ("After the Race"); one an event ("An Encounter"); and several a condition ("A Painful Case," "Grace," "The Dead"). The directness of most of them is deceptive, but a handful are highly elliptical and ambiguous. Irony informs "Two Gallants," where gallantry is decidedly unobservable; that it is Ivy Day during the course of the political tale arranged for ironic contrast with the diluted Parnellism of the canvassers. "Grace" as well is intentional overstatement, for few would consider either Mr. Kernan or any of the others in a state of grace despite their presence in the Gardiner Street Church, although Kernan may in fact be in a state of animated suspension, during a period of grace. "Clay" offers various possibilities in the literal substance brought forth and withdrawn during the game: its applicability to the malleable character of the unfortunate Maria and its symbolic import as a designator of the condition of death, prefigured as such in the Byron poem that Chandler attempted to read. "Counterparts" is itself a counter of various parts, contrasting Farrington with each of his adversaries throughout, from Mr. Alleyne to Weathers to his son Tom, and extending outward to counterpartite applicability to the Chandler of the preceding story, where "A Little Cloud" both parallels the person of Little Chandler and a condition that marks him and affects him. That "The Sisters" deflects attention away from the dead priest to his surviving sisters indicates the Joycean method of narrative counterpoint, as also in the case of "The Dead," a story in which two sisters figure prominently. The possibility for interexchange of the titles of the first and last story offers a circular construct for Dubliners, a cycle that Joyce artistically quadratures in his gnomic parallel structures, squaring the circle, encircling the numerous squares.

—Bernard Benstock, "The Gnomonics of Dubliners." *Modern Fiction Studies* 34 (Winter 1988): pp. 519–539. ℗

## S. L. GOLDBERG ON VIRTUES AND LIMITATIONS IN *DUBLINERS*

> [Here S. L. Goldberg examines *gnomon* and *simony,* with *Stephen Hero* as a comparative background, to discuss the moral conditions prevalent in many of Joyce's short texts. In particular, Goldberg considers these designations as they relate to specific characters in *Dubliners* and as they suggest a metaphor of lightness and darkness in each text.]

The terms "paralysis" and "simony" (more discursively defined in *Stephen Hero*) suggest the pervasive moral condition, the "maleficent and sinful being," exposed in story after story. "Gnomon" suggests their artistic method, by which the whole is suggested by the part or (as with the gnomon on a sundial) the light by its shadow: the simple but effective metaphor of light/darkness is used in many of the stories.

In this first story, the old priest's physical paralysis becomes the mark of his failure of courage before the divine mystery he had tried to serve, and of his consequent resignation to hopelessness and death. In "An Encounter," the paralysis is that of diseased obsession. The unruly, romantic, adventurous spirit of the boy, seeking a larger freedom of life, encounters only the maleficent disorder of the old pervert; yet although he fears it, he outwits it: courage wins him his freedom. In "Araby," the boy's romantic longings at last collapse and yet triumph in the darkened hall of the bazaar; the chink of money and the inane chatter there come to represent the materialistic "simony" which (even in his own desires) at once betrays his foolish ideals and is itself exposed by their innocent "folly." And so on through the book. The stories become images: of paralysed automatism of the will, the paralysing hand of the past, a paralysing feebleness of moral imagination, a simoniacal willingness to buy and sell the life of the spirit, timidity, frustration, self-righteousness, fear of convention, fear of sin, hypocricy, vulgarity, pettiness. Each, with a fine dexterity, vivisects its material to lay bare the moral disease that distorts it to its present shape.

The metaphor of vivisection is Joyce's own, and it describes perfectly the art of such stories as "Two Gallants" or "Ivy Day in the Committee Room" or "Grace," an art swift, sharp, accurate, with every stroke deliberately measured. The tone is flat, grimly reticent;

the style distant; the observation and metaphorical detail so consistently pointed that they achieve a kind of wit. Yet the success is not consistent. Some stories are too intent upon their analytical purposes. The formal neatness of "Eveline," "After the Race," "The Boarding House," and "Counterparts," for instance, is so obvious and oversimplifying, that the art comes to seem almost programmatic. These stories lack the vital detail pressing against the author's scalpel, and they also lack the author's rather malicious enjoyment both of his material and of his skill in dealing with it, which enliven "Two Gallants," "Ivy Day," "Grace," or even "A Little Cloud," "Clay," and "A Mother." But then, as all these images of spiritual decay succeed each other, we may well begin to question the mood of the book generally. Is not its tone, indeed its whole attitude to life, perhaps too insistently, and too constrictingly, "vivisective"?

—S. L. Goldberg, "Virtues and Limitations" in *James Joyce's "Dubliners": A Critical Handbook.* Eds. James R. Baker and Thomas F. Staley (Belmont, Calif.: Wadsworth Publishing Company, Inc., 1969): pp. 29–35.

## PHILIP F. HERRING ON THE TRIALS OF ADOLESCENCE

[Author of *Joyce's Uncertainty Principle*, Philip R. Herring presents the three often-quoted words that open "The Sisters," the first short story in *Dubliners*. Herring contends that an understanding of *gnomon, paralysis*, and *simony* are necessary not only to understand "The Sisters" but also to appreciate the entire collection.]

Joyce's rhetoric of absence made its initial appearance on the first page of *Dubliners*, where we find the three words in italics generally accepted as key words for interpretation. (Most critics have said that they are keys to the first story alone; I say they are relevant to the entire collection.) While *paralysis*, the first key word, has been widely discussed, *gnomon*, the second one, has remained murky. The *OED* tells us that it is both a parallelogram with a smaller parallelogram missing in one corner and the pillar of a sundial, which tells time by casting part of a circle into shadow. One should give more credence to Euclidian usage, since in the story the boy's understanding is probably restricted to that, but Joyce surely knew that in both definitions the missing part is what is important, either as a space that defines a geometric shape or as a shadow that indicates the time of day. *Gnomon* signaled his creation of absences that readers must make speak if they are to gain insight into character, structure, and narrative technique. In Greek, γνώμων means "judge" or "interpreter," which might provide a fanciful etymological link between the reader as interpreter in *Dubliners* and that which is to be discovered—significant but suppressed meaning. The richness of *gnomon* is precisely its vagueness.

"Gnomonic" language may contain ellipses, hiatuses in meaning, significant silences, empty and ritualistic dialogue. We note the continual emphasis on emptiness, incompletion, solitude, loneliness, shadow, darkness, and failure, which so affect the lives of Joyce's Dubliners and allow subtle expression of his political views.

Joyce must have been well instructed in the dictionary meanings of gnomon, because the concept is relevant to most of the major concerns of *Dubliners*. It suggests that certain kinds of absence are typical of the whole of Dublin life at a significant time in its history. (Here the sundial meaning of the word is applicable.) In effect, a *gnomon* may be a key synecdoche of absence, part of a political rhetoric of silence within a larger framework of language. In general, it indicates how selective examples such as the characters of *Dubliners* define life in their city, how shades illuminate presences, even how abnormality can define the normal.

The third key word in the opening paragraph of "The Sisters" is *simony*, the buying and selling of ecclesiastical preferment. If *paralysis* describes the moral and physical condition of Dubliners, given their need for freedom, transcendence, and fulfillment, and *gnomon* reemphasizes these absences at a particular time in history, then *simony* points to corruption in high places and illegitimate ecclesiastical authority as the primary obstacles to people's fulfillment. The first two terms describe the condition, telling readers how to arrive at meanings deeper than the textual surface, while the word *simony* places the blame squarely where Joyce thought it belonged—on institutions and their representatives who barter sacred rights. Ambition, energy, free will, revolutionary zeal—these forces play no role and could not, Joyce thought, in a city and country where centuries of political and religious oppression had caused a general paralysis of mind and will. Transcendence came only through death or emigration.

— Philip F. Herring, "*Dubliners*: The Trials of Adolescence" in *James Joyce: A Collection of Critical Essays.* Ed. Mary T. Reynolds (Englewood Cliffs, N.J.: Prentice-Hall, Inc., 1993): pp. 67–80.

## PATRICK PARRINDER ON SYMBOLISM IN *DUBLINERS*

[In this excerpt, the British scholar Patrick Parrinder reviews briefly the historical background of Symbolism as a literary theory. Professor Parrinder explains the theory in the context of *Dubliners* and in terms of Joyce's literary contemporaries. Parrinder concludes that symbolic interpretation must be viewed only as "an aid to understanding" in conjunction with other reading methodologies.]

Symbolism was described by Arthur Symons in 1899 as "a form of expression, at the best but approximate, . . . for an unseen reality apprehended by the consciousness." Like naturalism, the symbolist movement in literature was a late nineteenth-century import from France. The theory of epiphanies . . . is indebted to both naturalist and symbolist doctrines. Joyce's readers, however, did not encounter this theory until 1944, when *Stephen Hero* was published. The same year saw the publication of a scholarly article offering—I believe for the first time—an esoteric interpretation of *Dubliners*. Richard Levin and Charles Shattuck argued in "First Flight to Ithaca" that *Dubliners* like *Ulysses*, incorporated an elaborate structure of allusions to Homer's *Odyssey*. The Homeric allusions made up a consistent layer of meaning which, they claimed, no earlier reader had spotted. This theory has been received, for the most part, in stunned silence. For one thing, it can neither be proved nor refuted. Seamus Deane, speaking in general terms, has written that "Many of the coincidences that surround Joyce's work seem entirely accidental." But who knows which are and which aren't? A later symbolic interpretation of

"Clay," by Marvin Magalaner, drew the fire of no less formidable an enemy than Stanislaus Joyce. "I am in a position to state definitely that my brother had no such subtleties in mind when he wrote the story," Stanislaus pronounced. I cannot resist quoting Magalaner's reply, a little gem of scholarly self-importance:

> This type of personal-acquaintance criticism is understandably dangerous. What family of a deceased writer has not felt that blood relationship and lifelong closeness afforded deeper insight into the writer's work than detached criticism could? This is a natural and healthy family tendency; . . . at the same time, one may suspect critical judgments enunciated by such sources as the last word on, say, literary symbolism.

It might equally be asked if here are any known cases of symbolic interpretations of literary works being withdrawn as a result of criticism. But nobody in this largely conjectural area will ever have the last word. Even Stanislaus Joyce accepted the presence of parodic allusions to Dante's *Divine Comedy* in "Grace," because his brother told him they were there.

Symbolism was a topical and widely discussed literary technique when Joyce was writing *Dubliners*. Yeats had been acclaimed by Arthur Symons as the leading English symbolist. Baudelaire's famous poem "Correspondences," with its evocation of Nature as a temple filled with "forests of symbols," had first appeared fifty years earlier. Baudelaire had been followed by the *symboliste* school of poets expounded by Symons, and also by a school of symbolist painters. Wilde's statement in the preface to *Dorian Gray*—"All literature is both surface and symbol"—had done much to familiarize the concept. Later historians such as Edmund Wilson would regard symbolism and naturalism as opposing tendencies, thanks to their polemical association with the doctrines of spiritualism and materialism respectively. Yet Flaubert and Zola are inveterately symbolic novelists, and Ibsen's symbolic mode is a crucial presence behind Joyce's story "The Dead". . . .

Symbolic interpretation is an aid to understanding *Dubliners* so long as it is not pursued in isolation from other modes of reading. Just as Stephen Dedalus rested his theory of beauty on the epiphany or spiritual manifestation, each of the *Dubliners* stories works towards an intuitive and unparaphraseable insight into reality.

—Patrick Parrinder, "Dubliners," in *James Joyce*. Ed. Harold Bloom (New York: Chelsea House Publishers, 1986): pp. 254–255.

# RICHARD J. THOMPSON ON INITIATION AND VICTIMIZATION IN *DUBLINERS*

[Professor Thompson assigns a very high position of importance to Joyce's short ficiton in *Dubliners* for its "subtle psychological effect," drawing this conclusion in light of the short fiction of Daudet, Chekov, Gogol, and Flaubert. In this extract, Thompson focuses on Joyce's use of gaming and playing as evocations of initiation, tribulation, and victimization in the Dubliners stories.]

One supposedly simple motif from *Dubliners* might be chosen to illustrate Joyce's interweaving artfulness and high craft, namely his use of the metaphor of gaming or playing, in its multiplicity of connotations, which is plaited through the book to organize character and signal character change, usually from innocence to the pain of mature insight. Thus Maloney, according to the old josser in "An Encounter," "is different; he goes in for games." Indeed, he goes in for chasing and stoning cats and "brandishing his . . . catapult," the last of which is sexual slang for the old josser's own perverted game. But the game image is crucial to the point of the story: the bookish narrator is different from the screaming yahoo Maloney and lucklessly like the repulsive oldster. Play is also used to presage an unpleasant realization in "Araby." There the narrator leaves behind the "career of [his] play" to confront the sobering bazaar of life and its seedy Café Chantant where the money-grubbers lurk. His bibulous and insincere uncle's bromide about "All work and no play" is a preparation for the general insincerity of the adult world. The lonely drudgery of Eveline's life in the story of that name—she forsakes marriage and children to wait on her whining widower father—is hinted at again through the image of play by Joyce when he tells us that Eveline used "to play every evening with other people's children." So will it be for her in perpetuity.

But Joyce goes on to use play or gaming to effect even larger suggestions than the encroaching tribulations of growing up. In "After the Race," during the card game on the Belle of Newport, Jimmy Doyle, standing for Ireland, is retired to the role of witless onlooker whose patrimony is usurped by the representatives of England and France ("Jimmy understood that the game lay between Routh and Segouin"). The card game becomes a re-enactment of Irish national history with Jimmy playing the part of the ultimate grand loser. From playing cards Joyce goes to playing music in "Two Gallants"— the weary harpist's one hand "played in the base the melody of *Silent, O Moyle*, while the other hand careered in the treble after each set of notes." The begging street artist's hand strokes but cannot excite: the image depicts the national state of the arts. This parodic gesture is caricatured by Lenehan when later he absently strokes the silent railings around the Duke's Lawn. Presumably, Corley is fondling the slavey at the same time. All loves are sordid in this story, all gold fool's gold, all music mute or dissonant. Going with decent girls, as Lenehan says, is "a mug's game."

Bob Doran is himself the game or quarry ("He had a notion he was being had") in "The Boarding House," though the "Madam" compounds the image when she counts all her "cards" before sending for him, feeling sure "she would win." In this story and others, playing becomes a metaphor for manipulating people into doing what one wants. Jack Mooney stands menacingly by to see that Polly gets her cracker, ensuring that no one will try "that sort of game on with his sister." In "A Little Cloud," Ignatius Gallaher is as calculating as the "madam," being resolved to avoid Little Chandler's failure in marriage by marrying someone wealthy ("See if I don't play my cards properly"), while Farrington in "Counterparts" loses his reputation as a strong man and his ideal of himself as a playboy when he loses the hand-wrestling game to the knockabout artiste, Weathers. His lost ability to drink, to hand-wrestle, to play in general, underscores the tackiness of his life.

—Richard J. Thompson, *Everlasting Voices: Aspects of the Modern Irish Short Story.* (Troy, N.Y.: The Whitson Publishing Company, 1989): pp. 7–8.

# Works by
# James Joyce

*Chamber Music*. London: Elkin Mathews, 1907.

*Dubliners*. London: Grant Richards, 1914.

*A Portrait of the Artist as a Young Man*. New York: B. W. Huebsch, 1916.

*Exiles*. London: Grant Richards, 1918.

*Ulysses*. Paris: Shakespeare & Company, 1922.

*Pomes Penyeach*. Paris: Shakespeare & Company, 1927.

*Finnegans Wake*. London: Faber & Faber; New York: Viking Press, 1939.

*Stephen Hero*. New York: New Directions, 1944.

*Collected Poems*. New York: Viking Press, 1957.

*Critical Writings*. Eds. Ellsworth Mason and Richard Ellman. New York: Viking Press, 1959.

*Giacomo Joyce*. Ed. Richard Ellman. London: Faber & Faber; New York: Viking Press, 1968.

*The James Joyce Archive*. Eds. Michael Groden et al. 63 vols. New York and London: Garland Publishing Co., 1978–1980.

*Letters*. Vol. I. Ed. Stuart Gilbert. London: Faber & Faber; New York: Viking Press, 1957. Vols. II–III. Ed. Richard Ellman. London: Faber & Faber; New York: Viking Press, 1966.

*Selected Letters*. Ed. Richard Ellman. London: Faber & Faber; New York: Viking Press, 1975.

*James Joyce's Letters to Sylvia Beach*. Eds. Melissa Banta and Oscar Silverman. Bloomington: Indiana University Press, 1987.

*Poems and Epiphanies*. Eds. Richard Ellman and A. Walton Litz. London: Faber & Faber; New York: Viking Press, 1990.

# Works about
# James Joyce

Attridge, Derek, ed. *The Cambridge Companion to James Joyce.* London and New York: Cambridge University Press, 1990.

Beja, Morris, ed. *James Joyce, Dubliners and A Portrait of the Artist as a Young Man: A Selection of Critical Essays.* London: Macmillan, 1973.

Bloom, Harold, ed. *James Joyce.* New York: Chelsea House, 1986.

——————, ed. *James Joyce's "Dubliners."* New York: Chelsea House, 1988.

Boyle, Robert. "Swiftian Allegory and Dantean Parody in Joyce's 'Grace.'" *James Joyce Quarterly* 7 (Fall 1969), 11–21.

Brown, Richard. *James Joyce and Sexuality.* Cambridge: Cambridge University Press, 1985.

Brown, Terrence. *Dubliners.* New York: Penguin, 1992.

Chestnutt, Margaret. "Joyce's *Dubliners*: History, Ideology, and Social Reality." *Eire-Ireland* 5 (September 1970), 45–66.

Cixous, Helene. "Joyce: The (R)use of Writing" in *Post-structuralist Joyce: Essays from the French.* Eds. Derek Attridge and Daniel Ferrer, 15–30. Cambridge: Cambridge University Press, 1984.

Davis, Joseph K. "The City as Radical Order: James Joyce's *Dubliners.*" *Studies in Literary Imagination* 3 (October 1970), 79–96.

Ellman, Richard. "Backgrounds of 'The Dead.'" *Kenyon Review* 20 (Autumn 1958), 507–28.

Fabian, David R. "Joyce's 'The Sisters': Gnomon, Gnomic, Gnome." *Studies in Short Fiction* 5 (Winter 1968), 187–89.

Fischer, Therese. "From Reliable to Unreliable Narrator: Rhetorical Changes in Joyce's 'The Sisters.'" *James Joyce Quarterly* 7 (Summer 1971), 85–92.

Foster, John. "Passage through 'The Dead.'" *Criticism* 15 (Spring 1973), 91–108.

Füger, Wilhelm. *Concordance to James Joyce's "Dubliners."* New York: Georg Olms, 1980.

Gifford, Don. *Joyce Annotated: Notes for "Dubliners" and "A Portrait of the Artist as a Young Man."* Berkeley: University of California Press, 2nd ed., 1982.

Hodgart, Matthew. *James Joyce: A Student's Guide.* London: Routledge & Kegan Paul, 1978.

Lane, Gary, ed. *A Word List to James Joyce's "Dubliners."* New York: Haskell House, 1972.

Magalaner, Marvin, ed. *A James Joyce Miscellany.* Third series. Carbondale: Southern Illinois University Press, 1962.

Mandel, Jerome. "Medieval Romance and the Structure of 'Araby.'" *James Joyce Quarterly* 13 (Winter 1976), 234–37.

Mikhail, E. H., ed. *James Joyce: Interviews and Recollections.* New York: St. Martin's Press, 1990.

Moynihan, William T., ed. *Joyce's "The Dead."* Boston: Allyn and Bacon, 1965.

Munich, Adrienne Auslander. "Form and Subtext in Joyce's 'The Dead.'" *Modern Philology* 82 (November 1984), 173–84.

Niemeyer, Carl. " 'Grace' and Joyce's Method of Parody." *College English* 27 (December 1965), 196–201.

Norris, Margot. "Stifled Back Answers: The Gender Politics of Art in Joyce's 'The Dead.'" *Modern Fiction Studies* 35, no. 3 (1989), 479–503.

Reynolds, Mary T. *Joyce and Dante: The Shaping Imagination.* Princeton: Princeton University Press, 1981.

Roberts, Robert P. " 'Araby' and the Palimpsest of Criticism; or, Through a Glass Eye Darkly." *Antioch Review* 26 (Winter 1966/67), 469–89.

Rosenburg, Bruce A. "The Crucifixion in 'The Boarding House.'" *Studies in Short Fiction* 5 (Fall 1967), 44–53.

Scholes, Robert, and A. Walton Litz, eds. *"Dubliners" Text, Criticism and Notes.* New York: Viking Press, 1969.

Senn, Fritz. " 'He Was Too Scrupulous Always': Joyce's 'The Sisters.'" *James Joyce Quarterly* 2 (Winter 1965), 66–72.

Sosnoski, James J. "Story and Discourse and the Practice of Literary Criticism: 'Araby,' A Test Case." *James Joyce Quarterly* 18 (Spring 1981), 255–67.

Staley, Thomas F. *An Annotated Critical Bibliography of James Joyce.* New York: St. Martin's Press, 1989.

Torchiana, Donald T. "The Ending of 'The Dead': I Follow Saint Patrick." *James Joyce Quarterly* 18 (Winter 1981), 123–33.

Walzl, Florence L. "Dubliners: Women in Irish Society" in *Women in Joyce.* Eds. Suzette Henke and Elaine Unkeless, 31–56. Urbana: University of Illinois Press, 1982.

# Index of
# Themes and Ideas